Waterford Ontario and Area in Colour Photos, Saving Our History One Photo at a Time

Photography
by Barbara Raué
2015

Series Name:
Cruising Ontario

Book 113: Waterford and Area

Cover photo: 163 Main Street, Waterford (Page 13)

Series Name: Cruising Ontario
Saving Our History One Photo at a Time
in colour photos

Books Available in Alphabetical Order:
Aberfoyle, Acton, Alton, Ancaster, Arthur, Aylmer, Ayr, Bloomingdale, Brantford, Burlington, Caledon, Caledonia, Cambridge, Clifford, Conestogo, Delhi, Dorchester to Aylmer, Drayton, Drumbo, Dundas, Eden Mills, Elmira, Elora, Fergus, Guelph, Hagersville, Hamilton, Hanover, Harriston, Hespeler, Jarvis, Kitchener, Linwood, Listowel, London, Lucknow, Mono, Mount Forest, Neustadt, New Hamburg, Niagara-on-the-Lake, Oakville, Orangeville, Orillia, Owen Sound, Palmerston, Peterborough, Port Elgin, Preston, Rockwood, Seaforth, Sheffield, Shelburne, Simcoe, Southampton, St. Jacobs, St. Thomas, Stoney Creek, Stratford, Tillsonburg, Waterdown, Waterrford, Waterloo, Wellesley, Wingham

Book 110:Lucknow, Mitchell
Book 111: Conestogo, Bloomingdale
Book 112: Delhi
Book 113: Waterford
Book 114-116: Waterloo
Book 117-119: Windsor

Other Books by Barbara Raue

Coins of Gold

Arrows, Indians and Love

The Life and Times of Barbara
Volume 1: Inventions That Have Enhanced My Life
Volume 2: Entertainment That I Have Enjoyed
Volume 3: East Coast Trips
Volume 4: Olympics Have Always Intrigued Me
Volume 5: Wonders of the World
Volume 6: Caribbean Cruises We Have Enjoyed
Volume 7: Animals
Volume 8: Storms and Other Major Disasters in My Lifetime
Volume 9: Wars, Terrorist Attacks and Major Disasters

The Cromwell Family Book

Laura Secord Discovered

Visit Barbara's website to view all of her books
http://barbararaue.ca

Waterford

Waterford is located on Pleasant Ridge Road, or old Highway 24 in Norfolk County, south of Brantford, north of Simcoe and southwest of Ohsweken. Waterford was established in 1794 with saw and grist mills on Nanticoke Creek. An early major industry was the agricultural implement factory built by James Green, a local merchant. The area surrounding the town is primarily agricultural land with tomatoes, tobacco and corn among the main crops. With the decline of the tobacco industry, area farmers have suffered, but ginseng is being grown on some farms. In 1979 a freak tornado swept through the town, knocked down trees, and damaged houses and public property.

Ohsweken

Ohsweken is a village on the Six Nations of the Grand River First Nation Indian Reserve. It is located on Chiefswood Road and 4th Line, southeast of Brantford. The six nations are Mohawk, Oneida, Onondaga, Cayuga, Seneca and Tuscarora.

Hartford

Hartford is located on Norfolk Country Road 74 and Highway 19 just south of the Indian Reserve.

Bealton

Bealton is located on Villa Nova Road and Highway 19.

Boston

Boston is located on Highway 4, Cockshutt Road and Highway 19.

Oakland

Oakland is located on Highway 24 and Regional Road 4, northeast of Waterford and southwest of Brantford.

*****

Table of Contents

Waterford

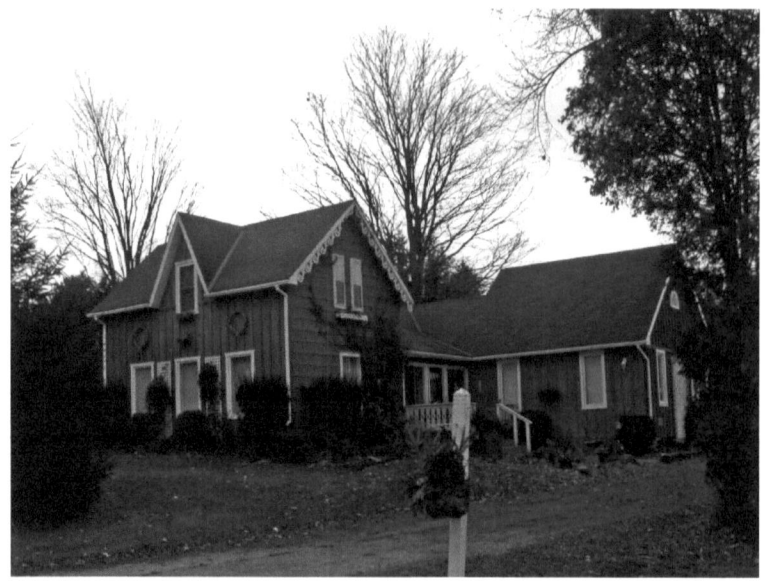

Gothic Revival, verge board trim on gable

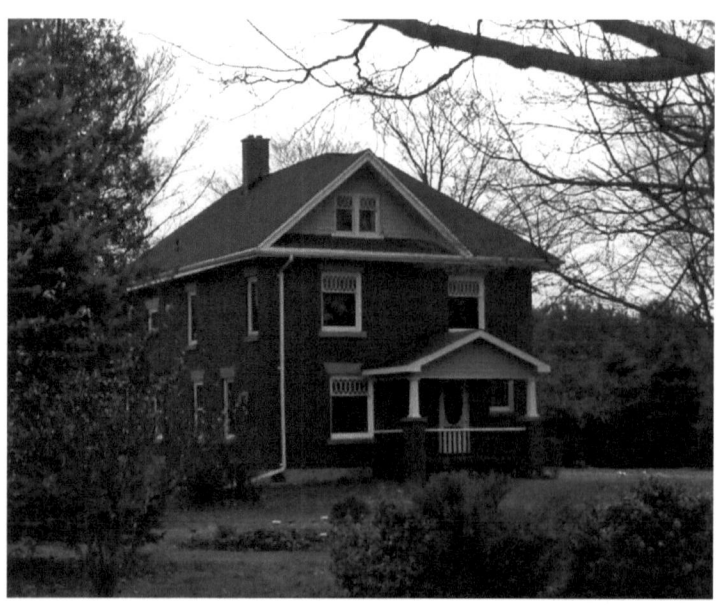

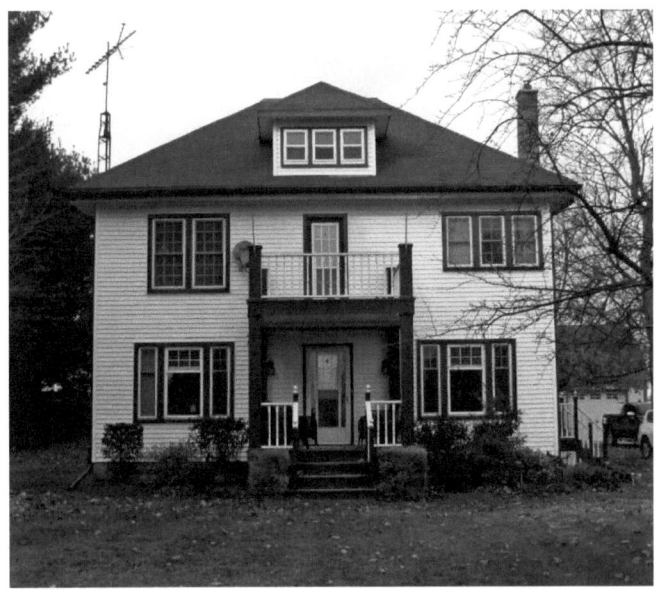

Italianate, hipped roof, dormer, second floor balcony

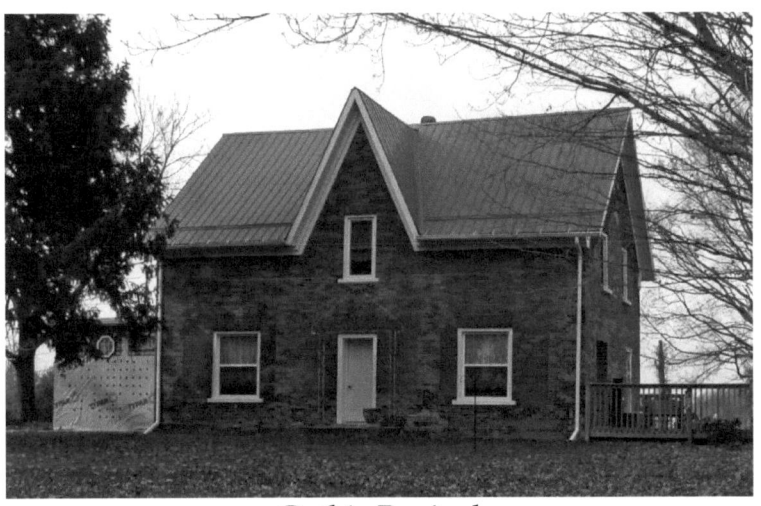

Gothic Revival

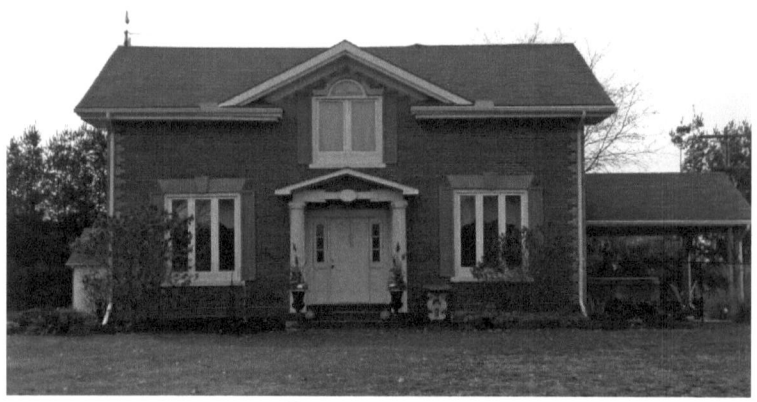

Corner quoins

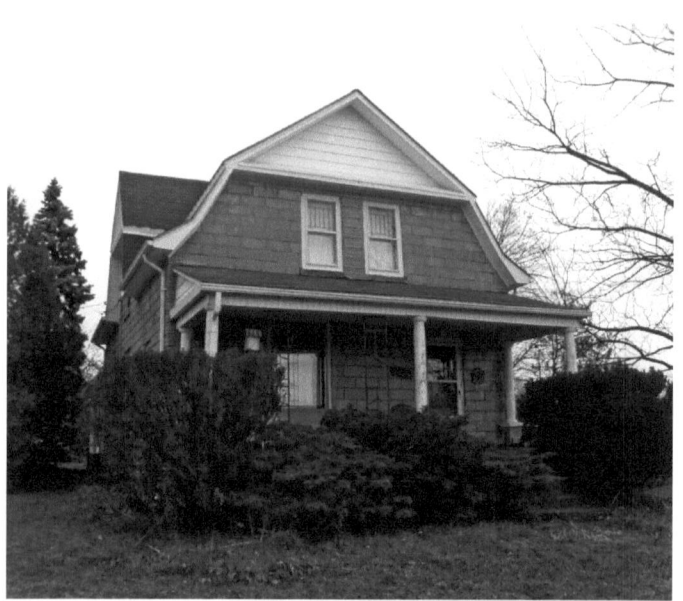

Cape Dutch style of architecture

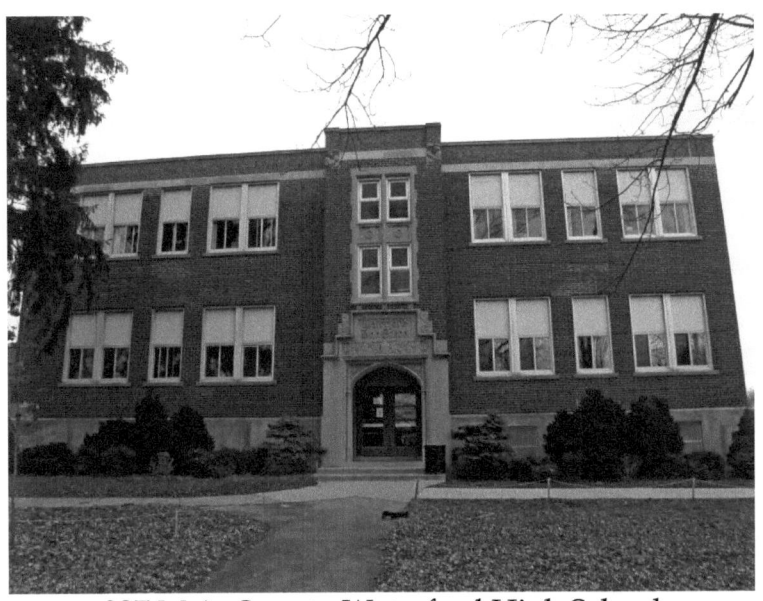

227 Main Street - Waterford High School
1892, 1931, 1936

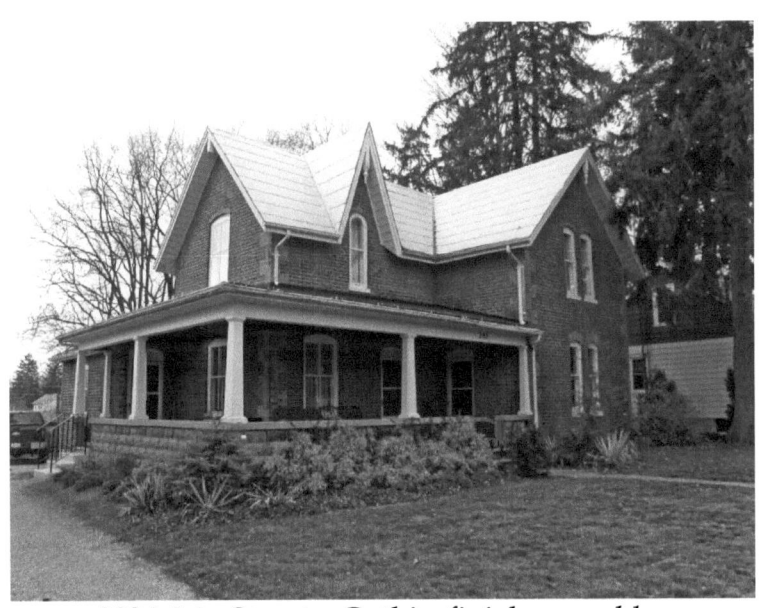

202 Main Street – Gothic, finials on gables

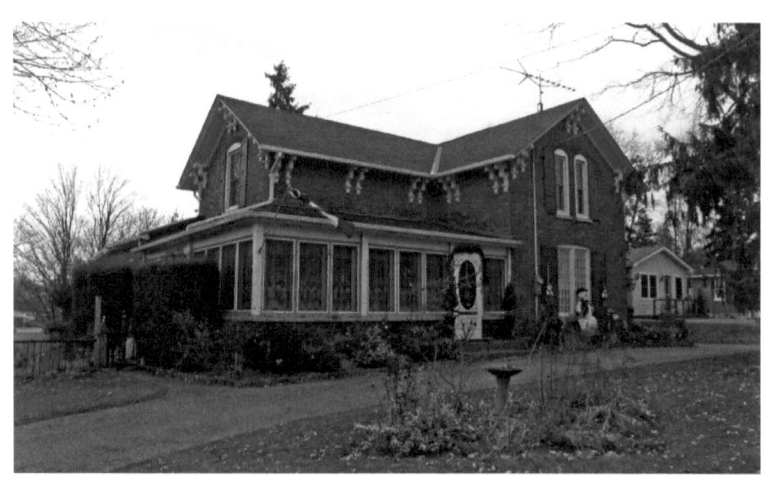

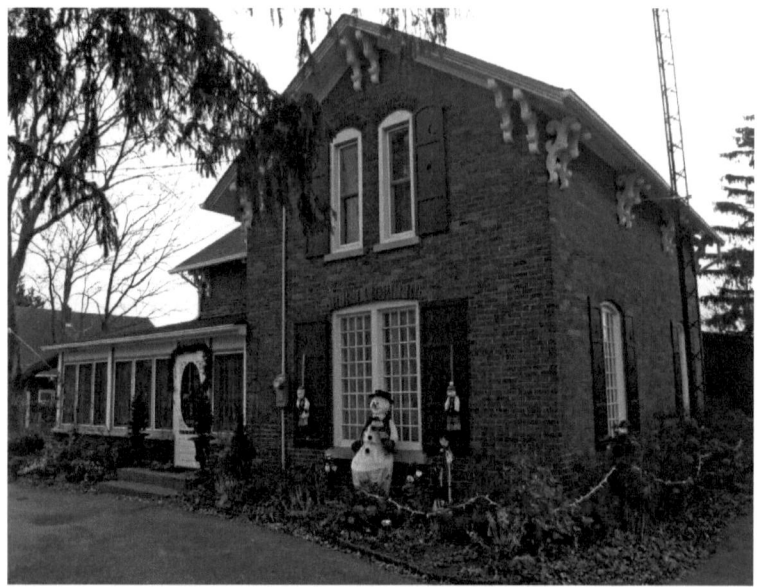

Gothic – paired cornice brackets

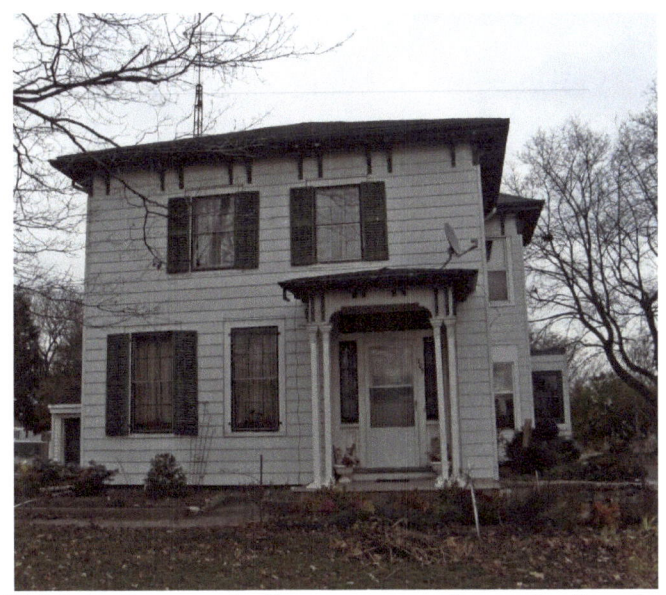

205 Main Street – Italianate, paired cornice brackets

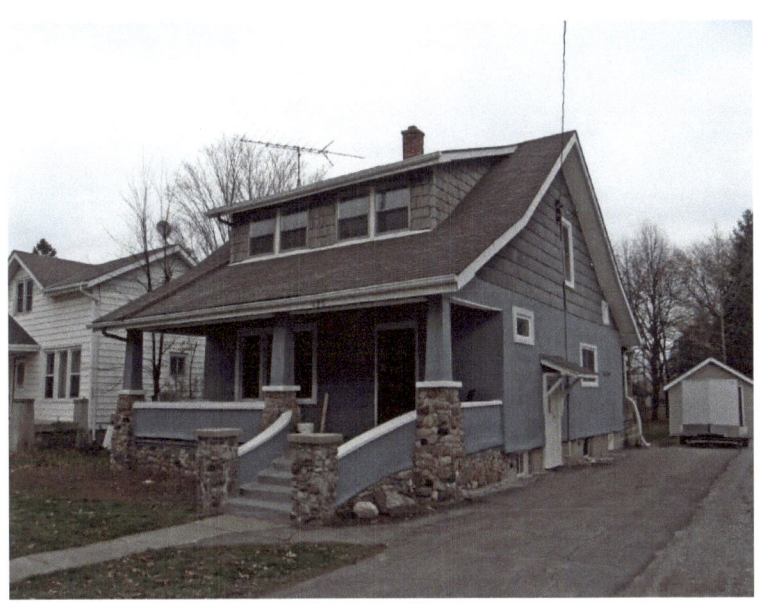

195 Main Street

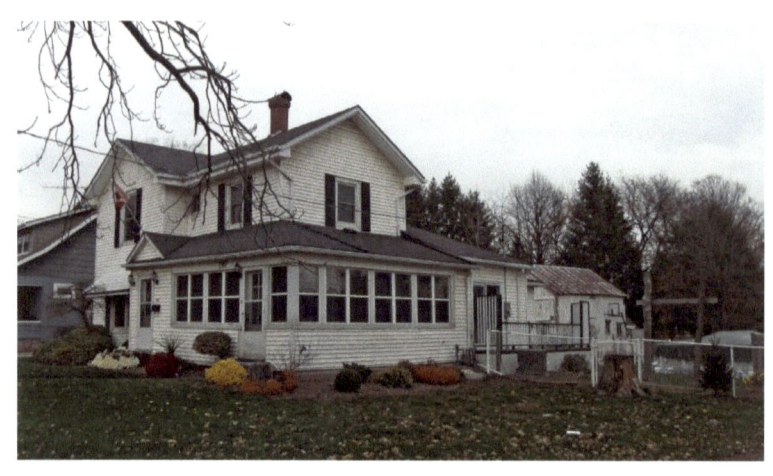

199 Main Street

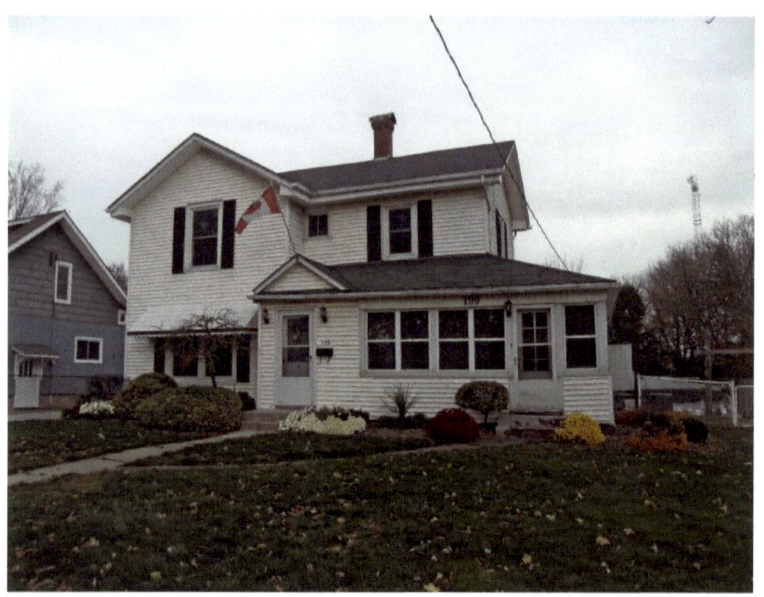

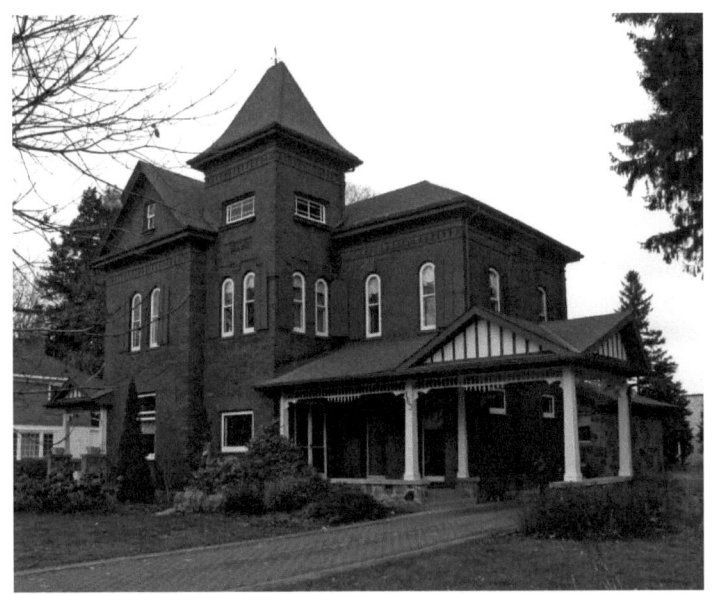

163 Main Street – Vernacular – three storey tower

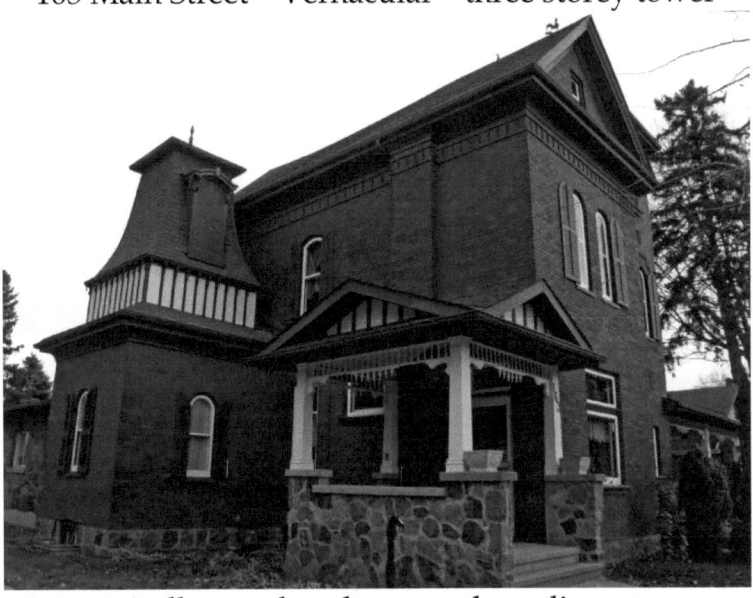

Intricate spindle woodwork on porch, pediments, unusual
shaped turret or tower

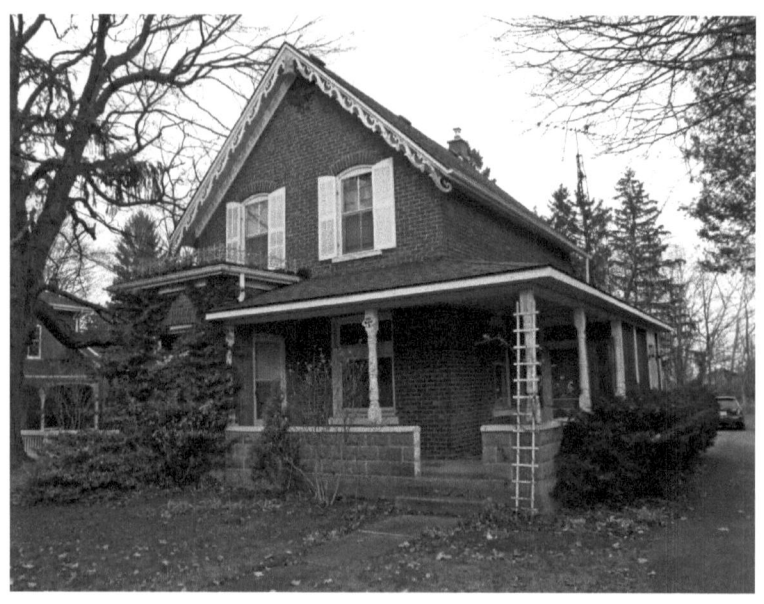

181 Main Street – Gothic Revival, verge board trim on gable

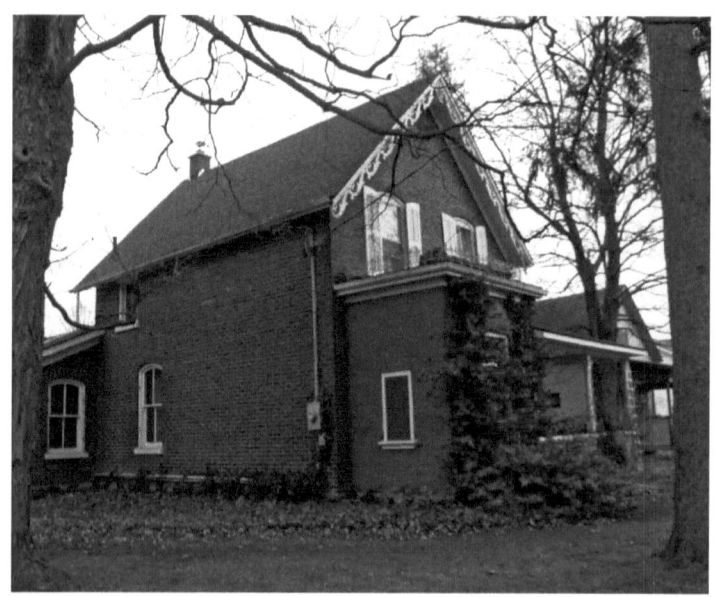

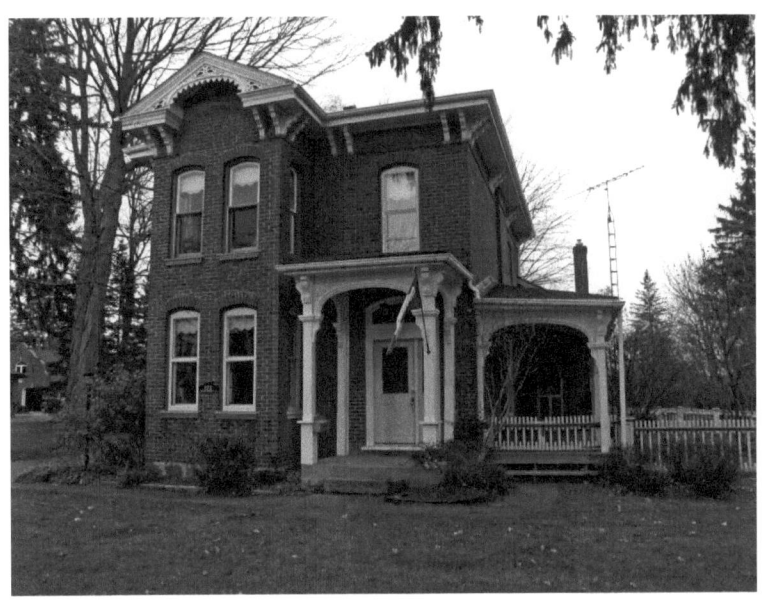

173 Main Street – two-storey tower-like bay capped with bargeboard trim on gable

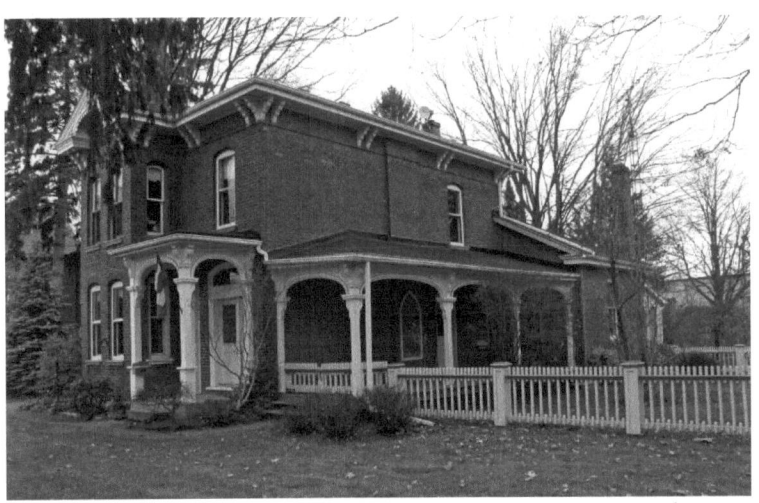

Italianate, paired cornice brackets, two-storey bay

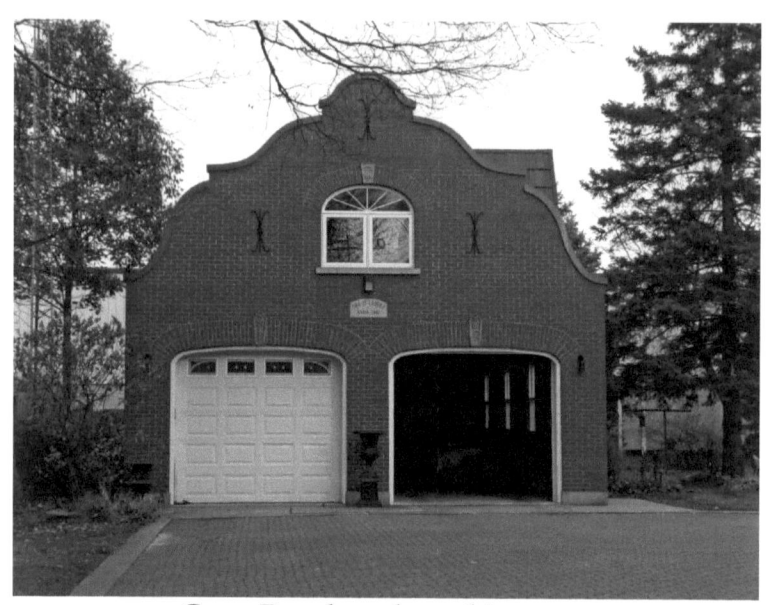

Cape Dutch style architecture

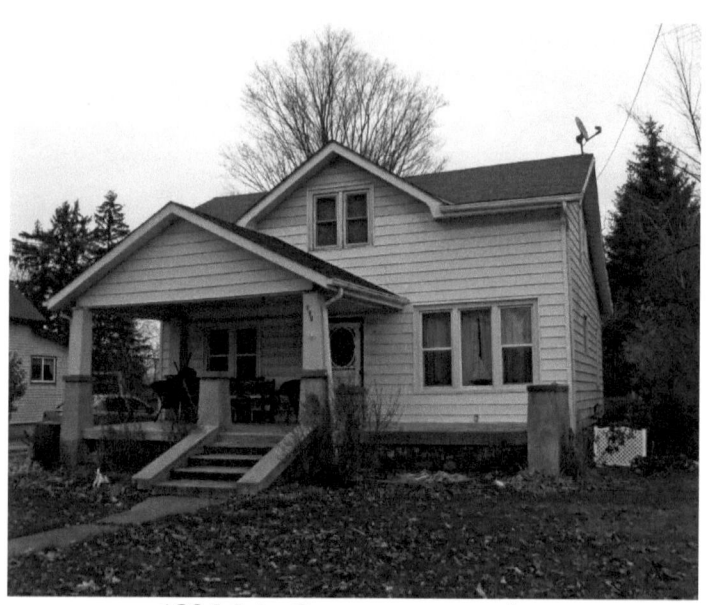

189 Main Street - vernacular

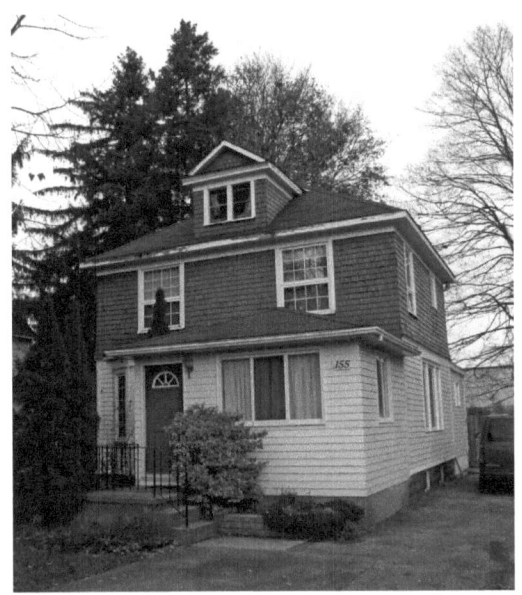

155 Main Street – hipped roof, dormer

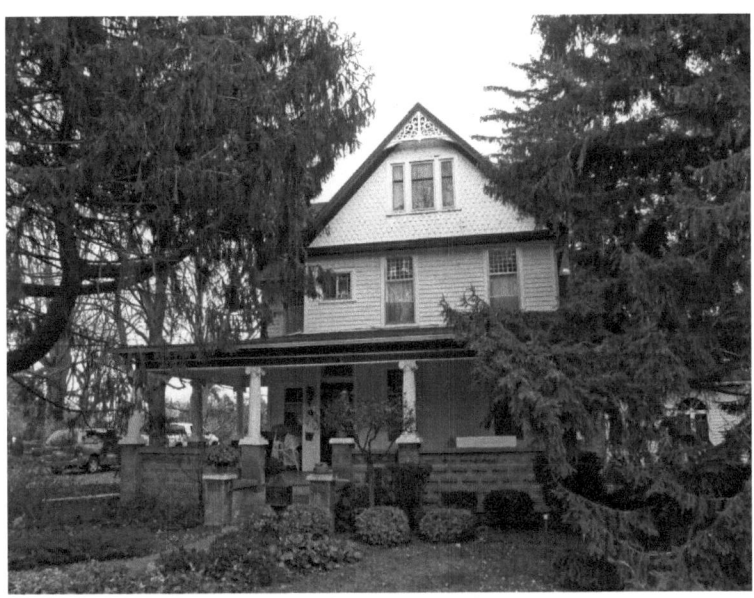

Gothic Revival

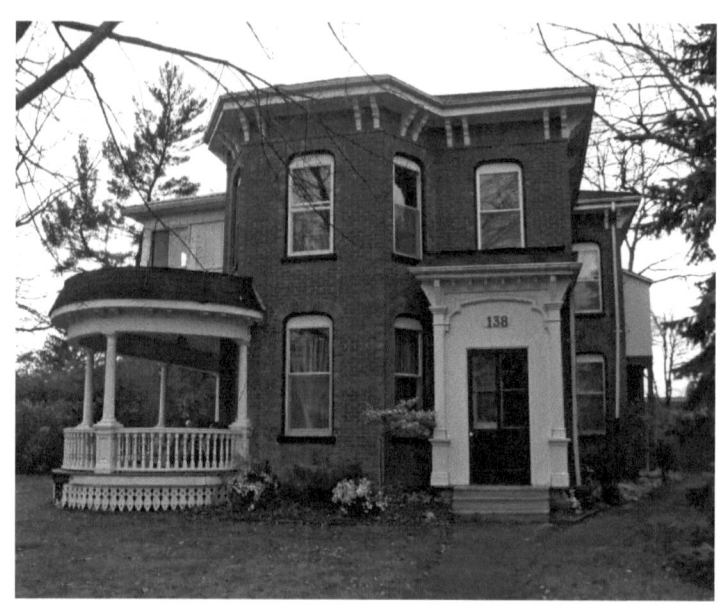

138 Main Street – Italianate, paired cornice brackets, wraparound verandah

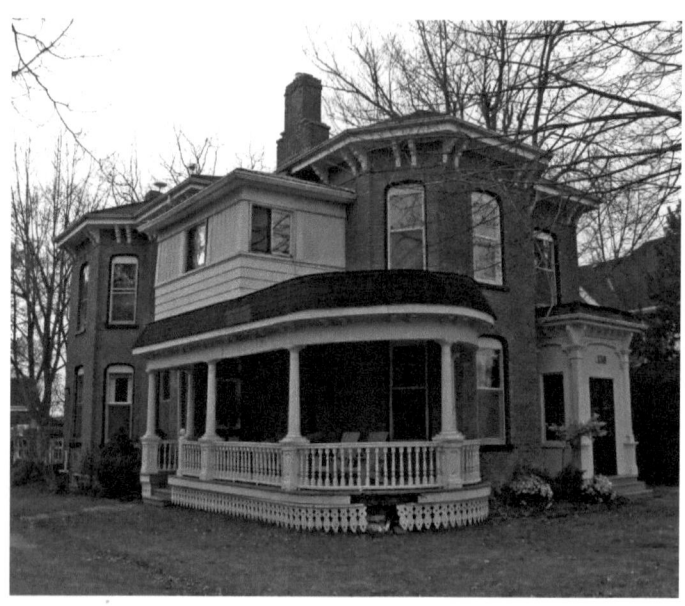

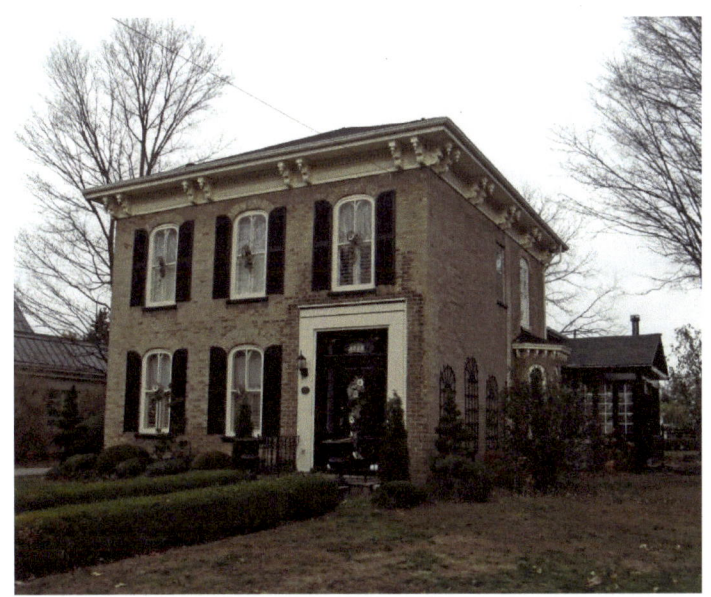

Italianate – paired cornice brackets, side bay window

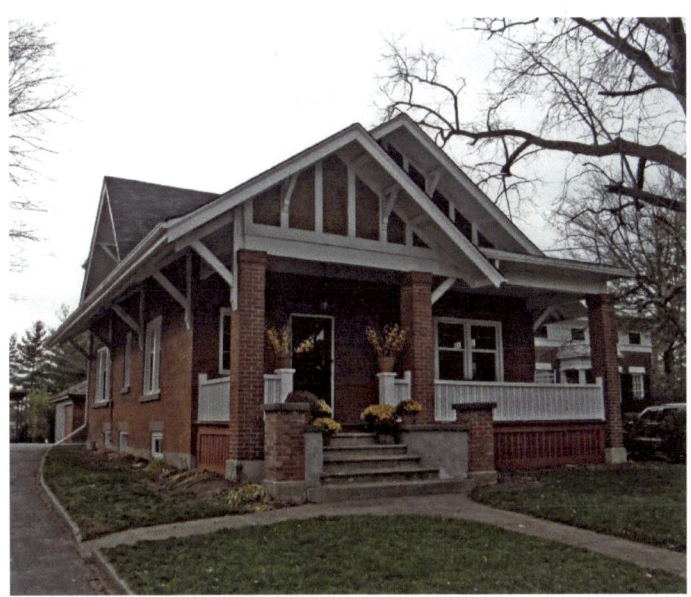

156 Main Street - Tudor

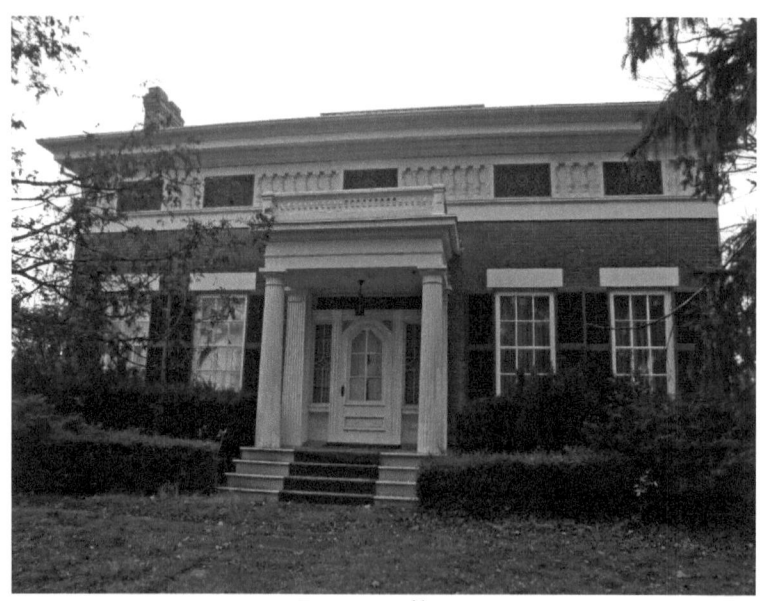

Doric pillars

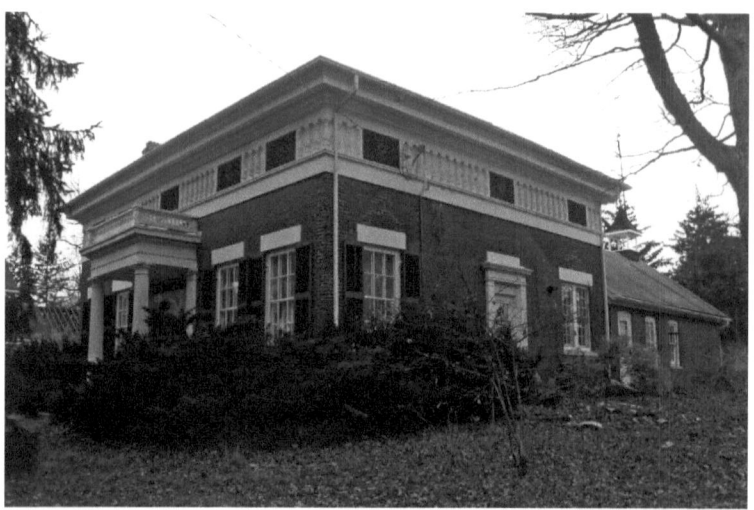

Italianate

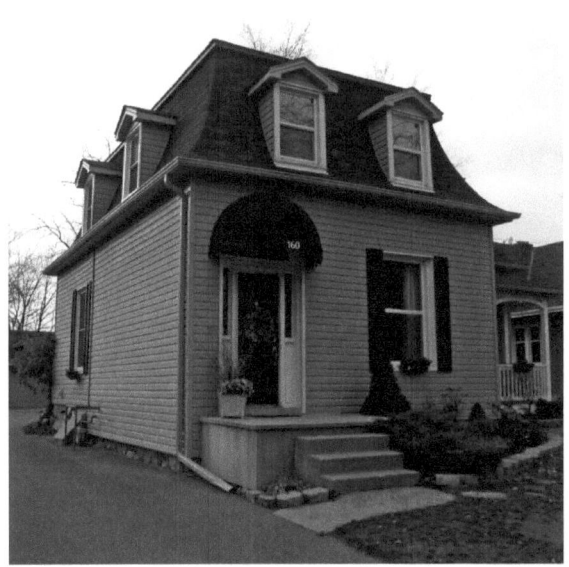

160 Main Street – Second Empire style, mansard roof, dormers

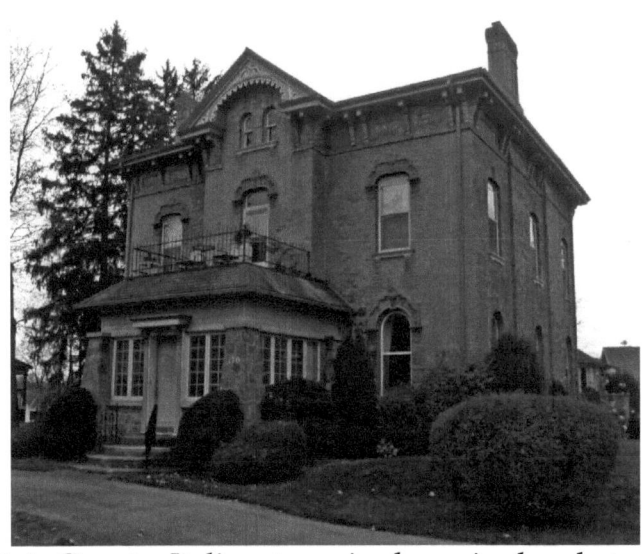

170 Main Street – Italianate, paired cornice brackets, barge board time with stenciling on gable, second floor balcony, Decorative voussoirs with keystones

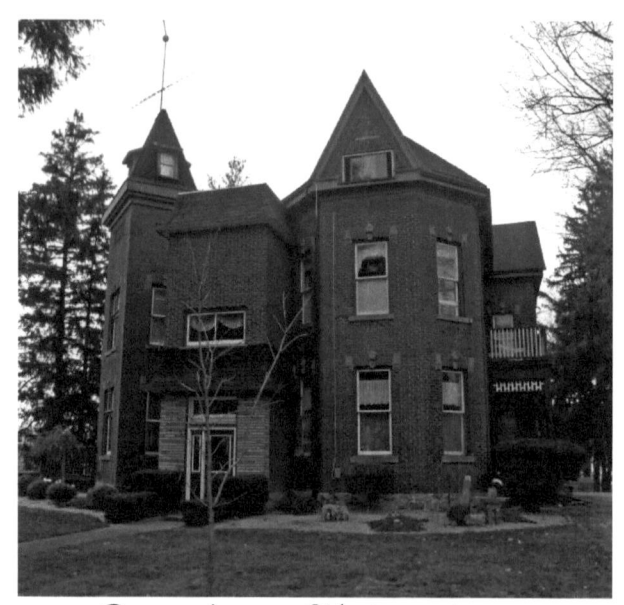

Queen Anne – 3½ storey tower

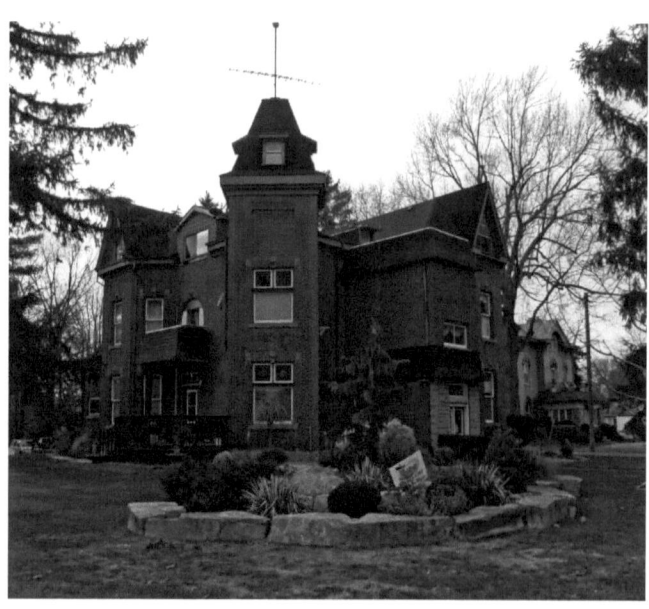

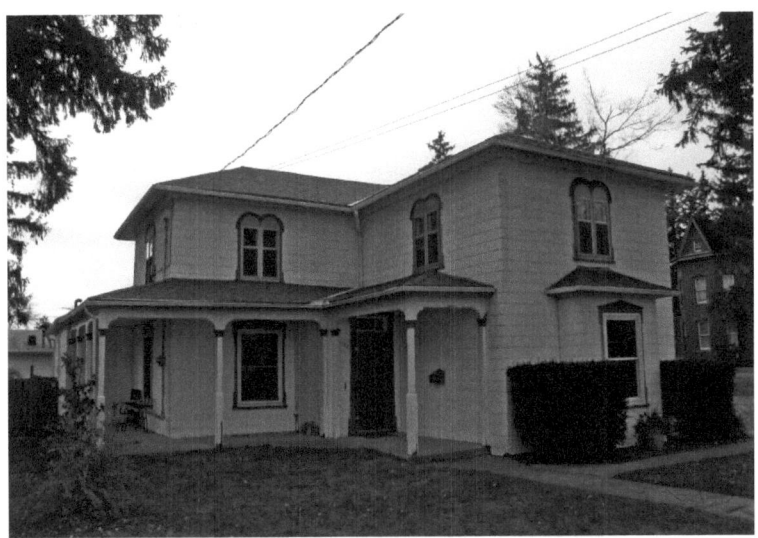

192 Main Street

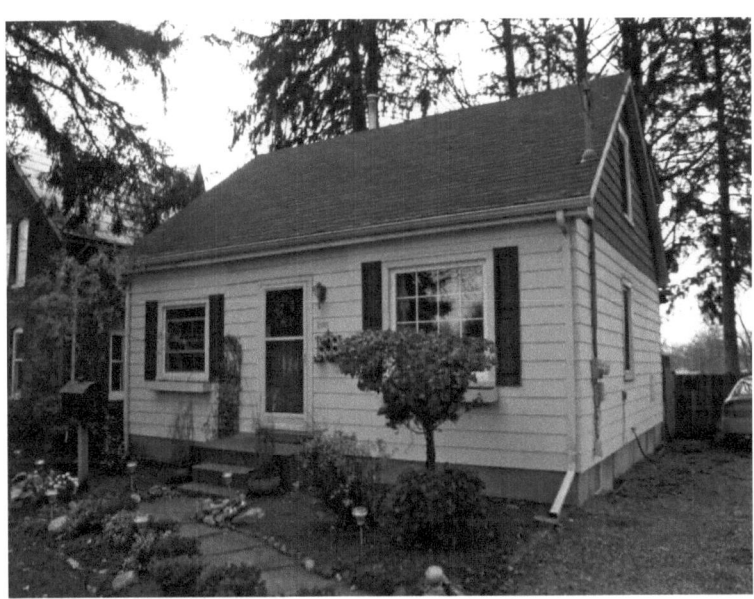

200 Main Street - Gothic

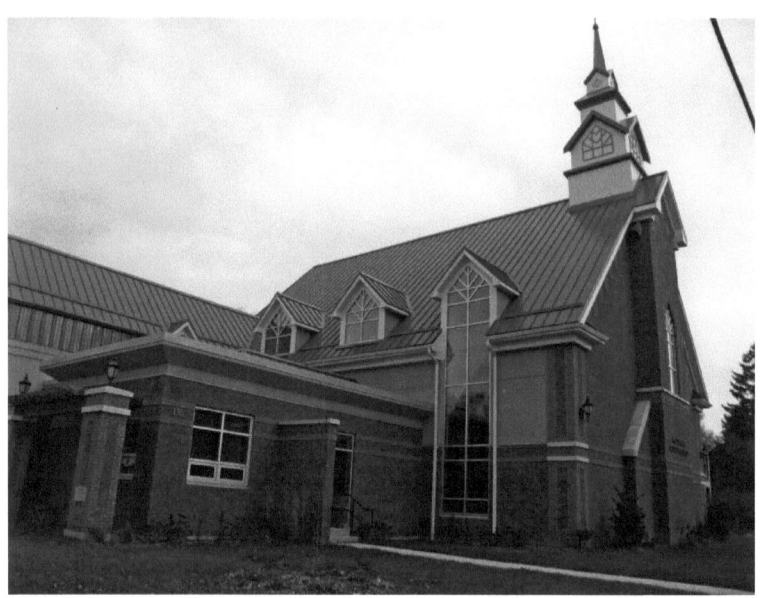

135 Main Street South - Waterford United Church rebuilt
2009-2010 (Methodist Church July 10, 1889)

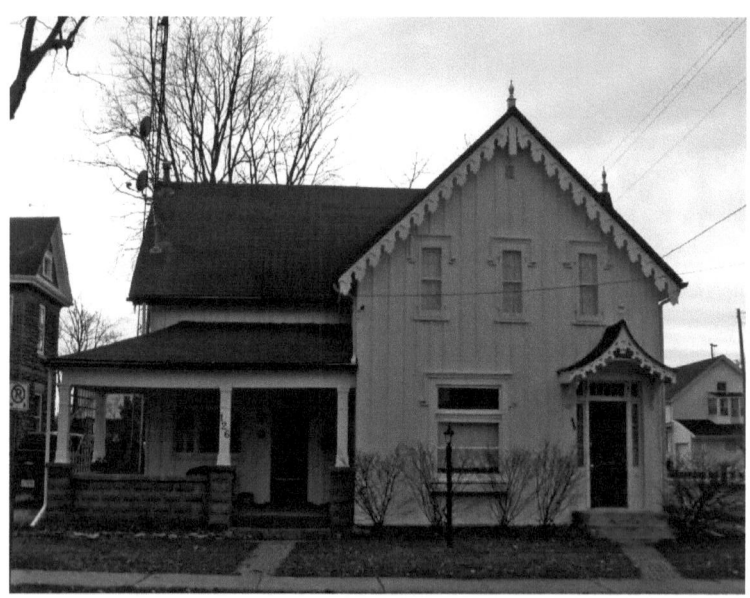

Gothic – verge board trim with finial on gable

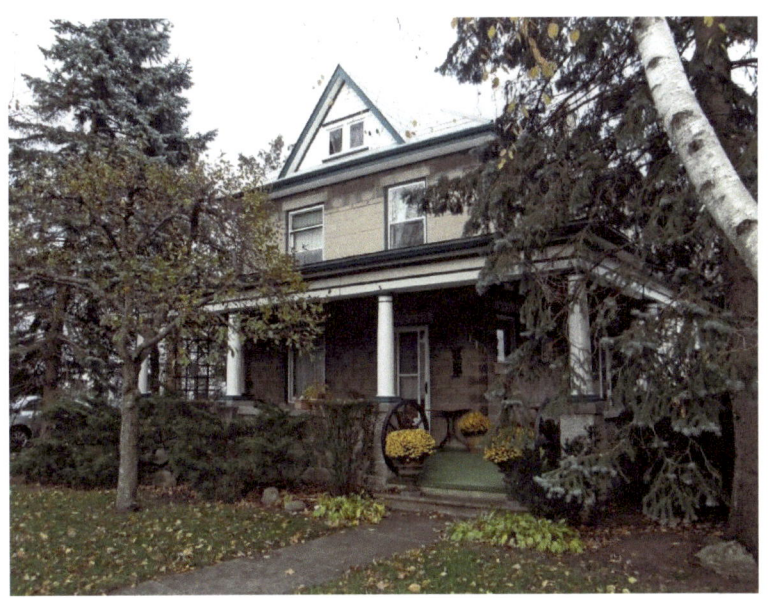

119 Main Street - Gothic

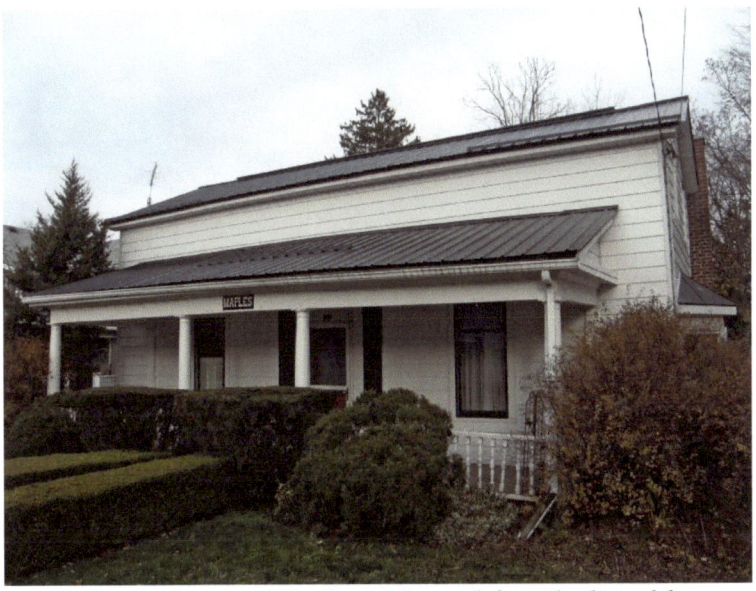

113 Main Street - Blacksmith and family lived here
in the late 1800s

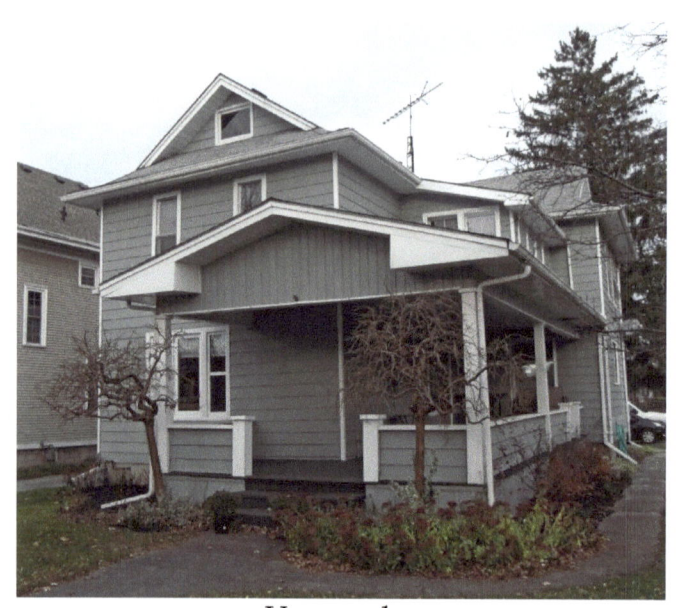

Vernacular

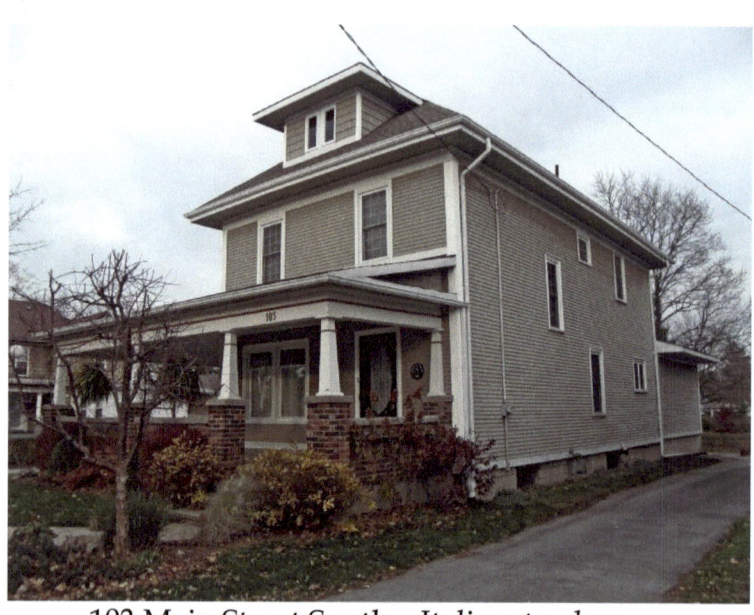

103 Main Street South – Italianate, dormer

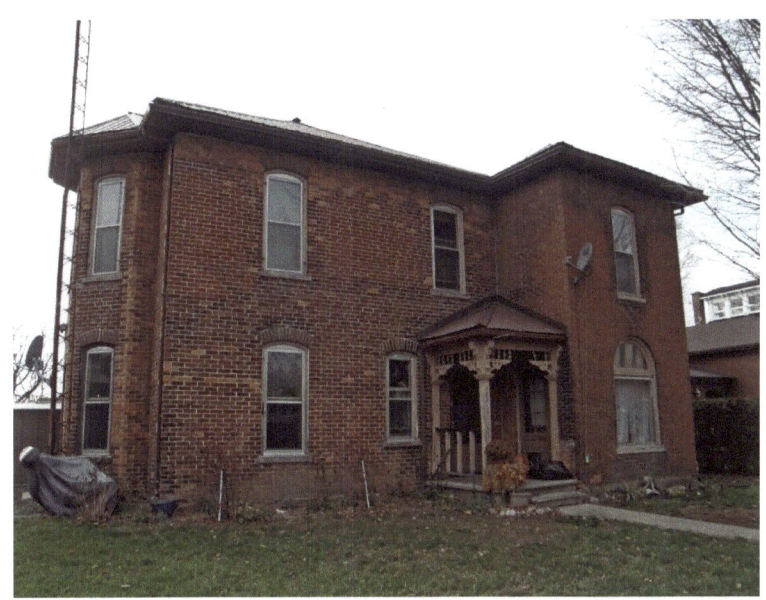

102 Main Street – spindles and intricate woodwork on porch supports

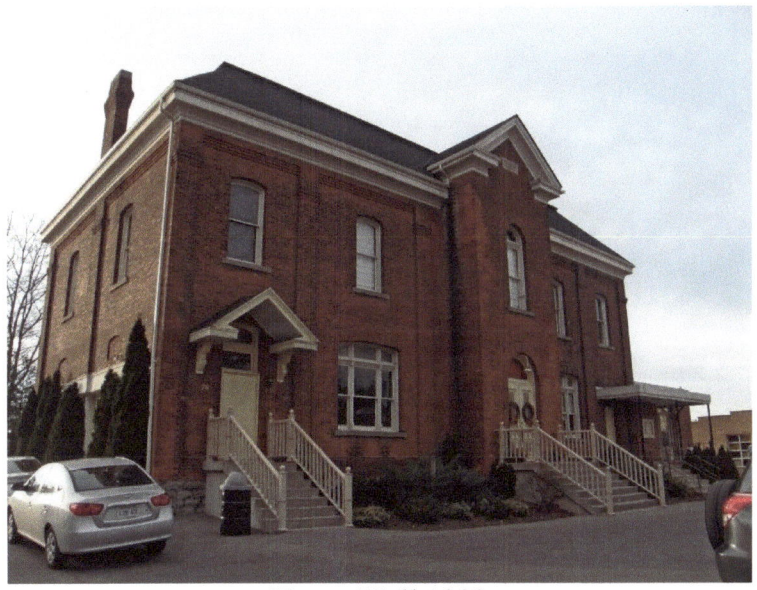

Town Hall 1902

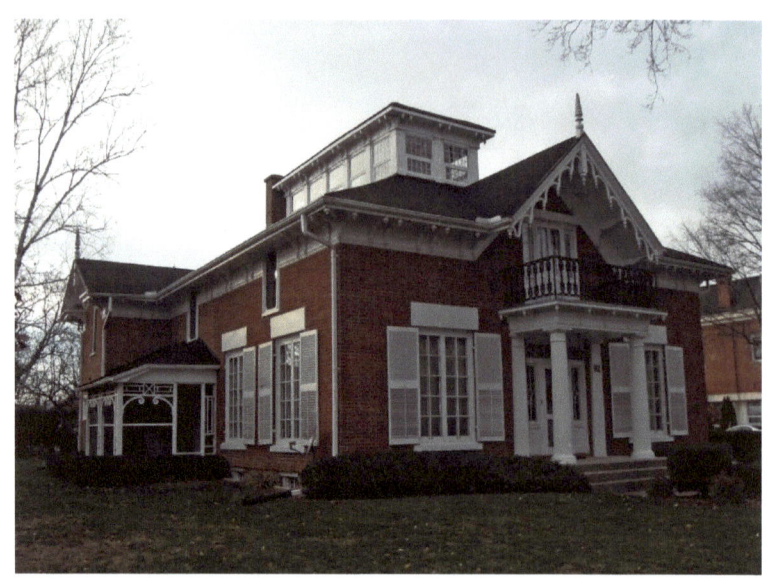

92 Main Street – Italianate, belvedere on roof, paired cornice brackets, verge board and finial on gables, second floor balcony, Doric columns

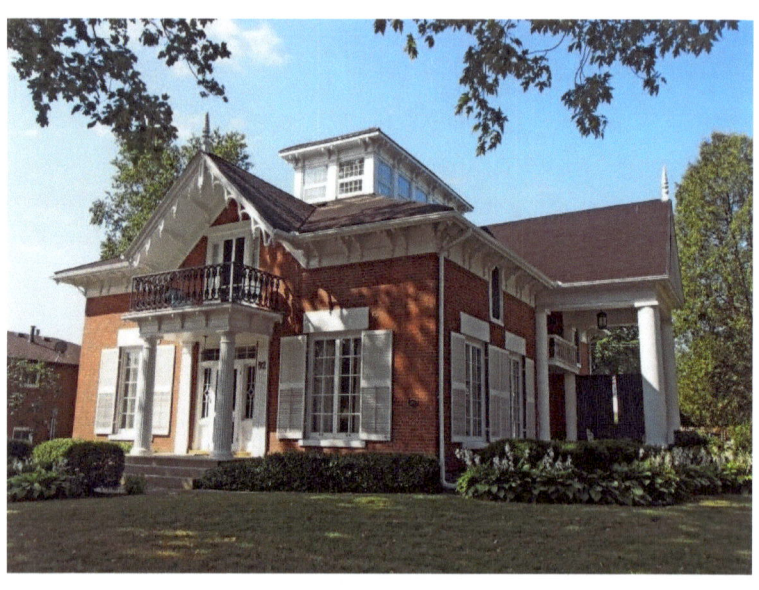

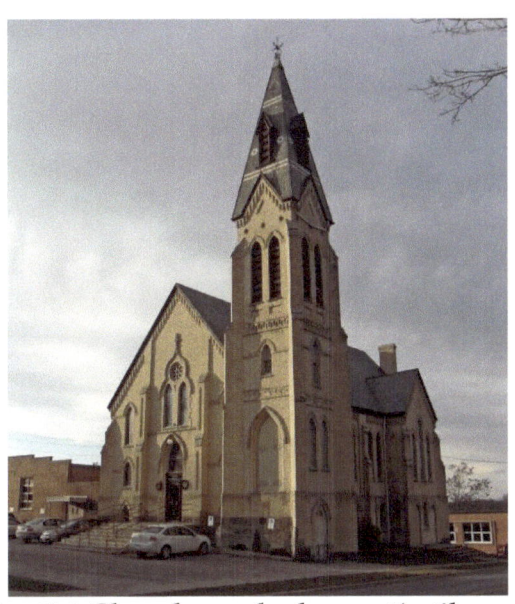

Waterford Baptist Church – polychromatic tilework on tower, bevelled dentil moulding, rose window, lancet windows, buttresses

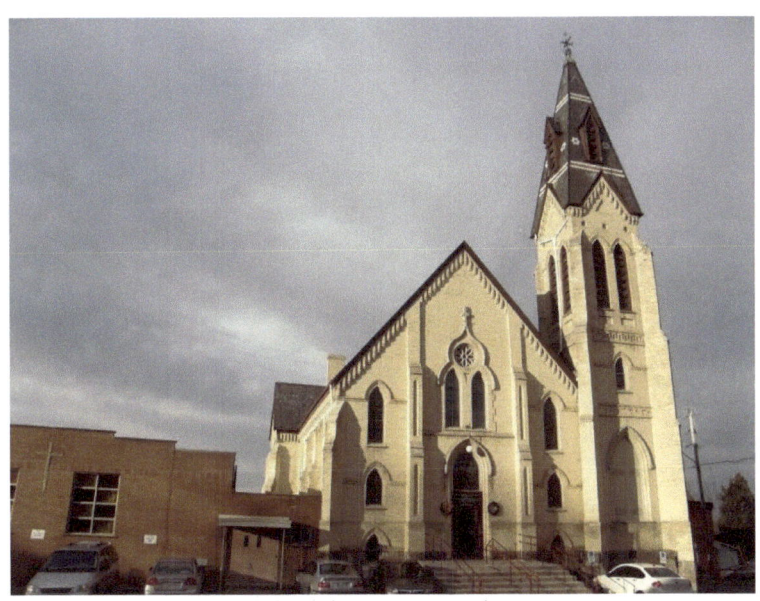

Gothic, lancet windows

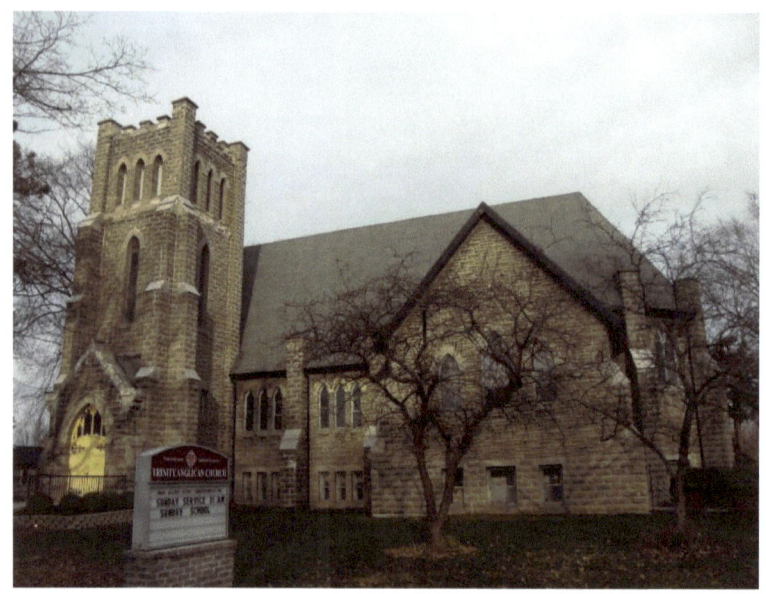

73 Main Street South - Trinity Anglican Church c. 1909
Crenelated tower

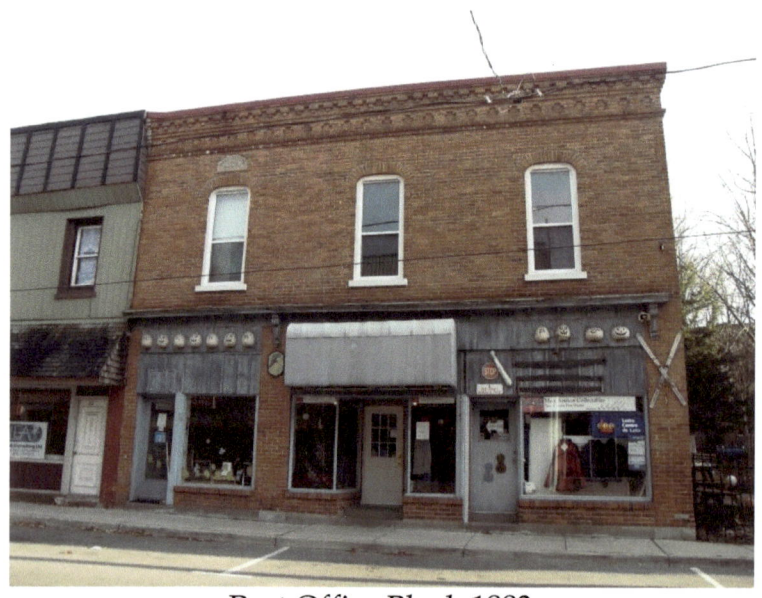

Post Office Block 1883

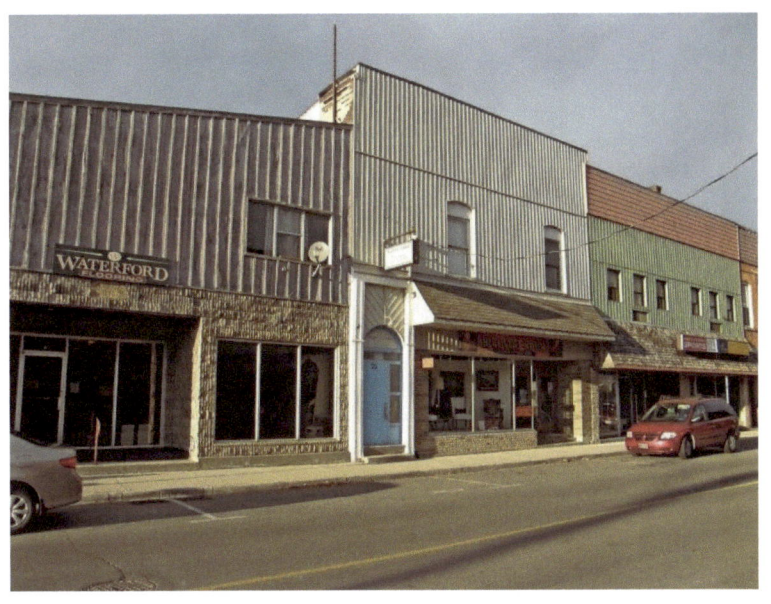

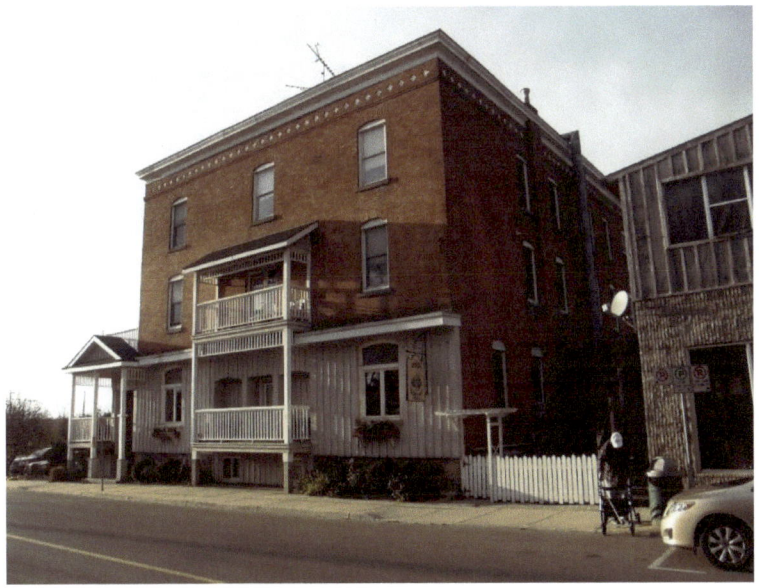

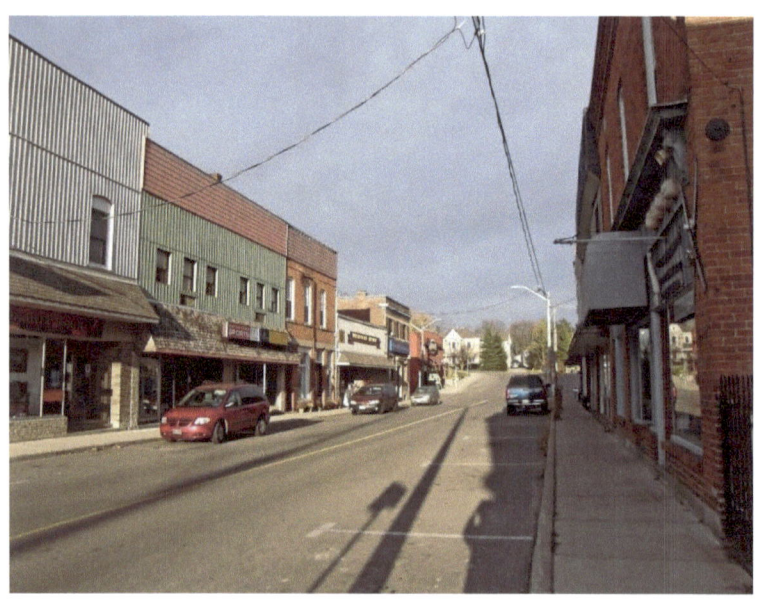

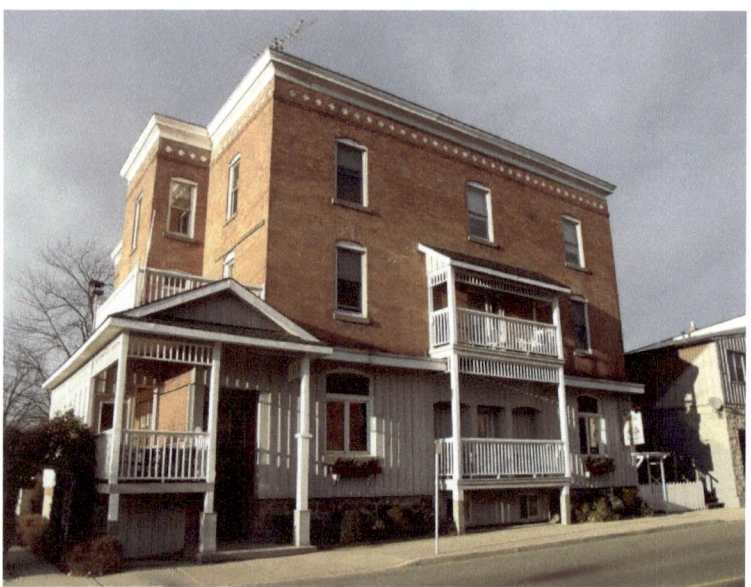

Patterned brickwork below cornice

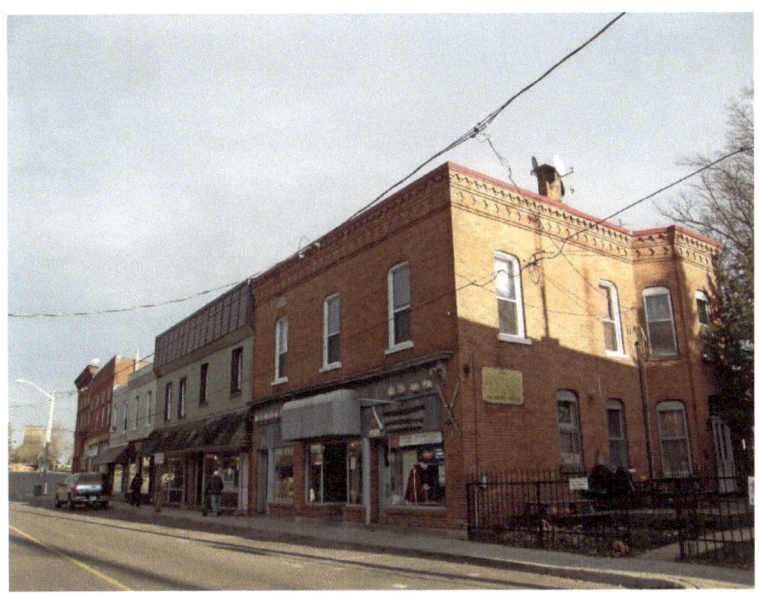

Bevelled dentil moulding

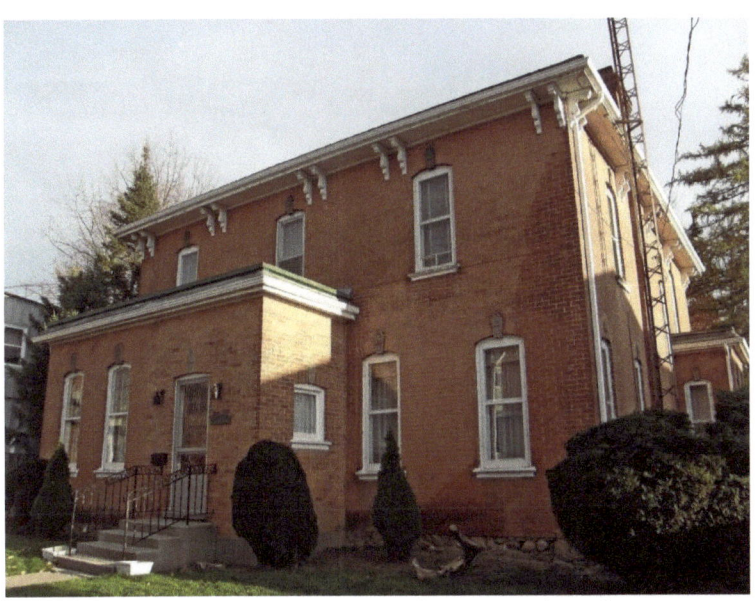

#44 – Italianate – paired cornice brackets

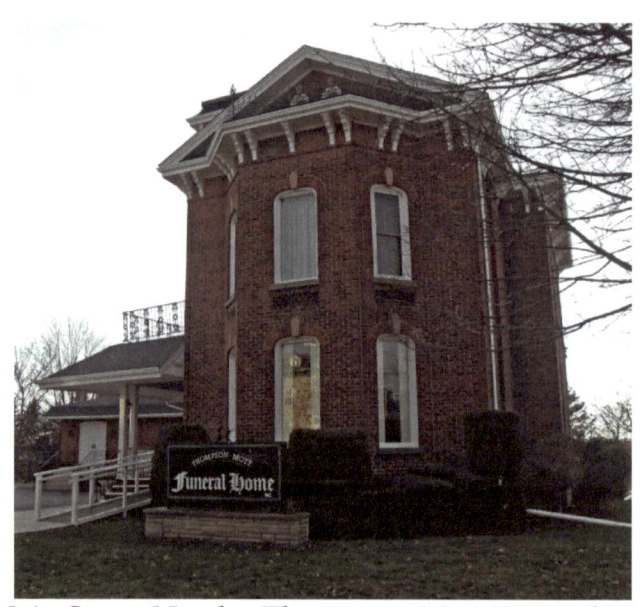

62 Main Street North - Thompson Mott Funeral Home, cornice brackets

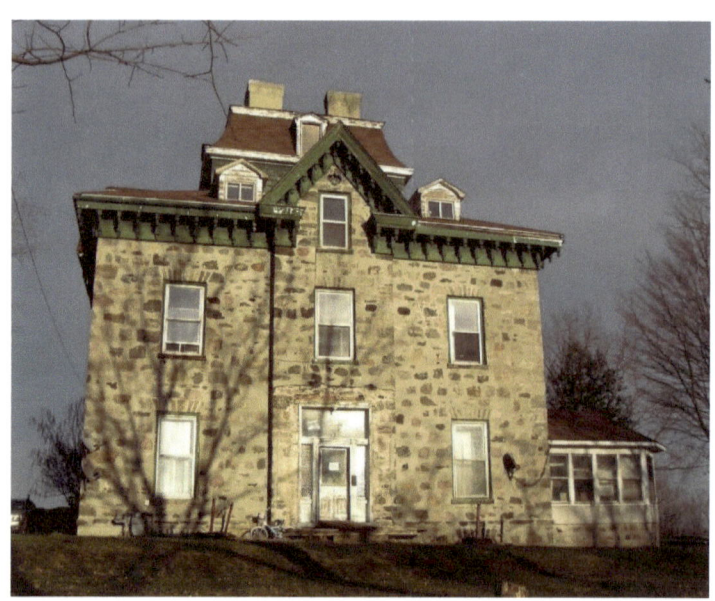

Cobblestone

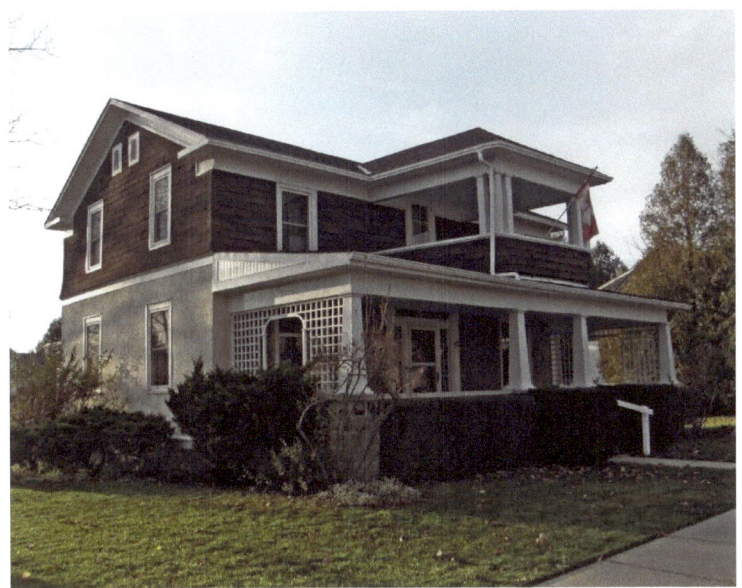

#72 – cornice return on gable

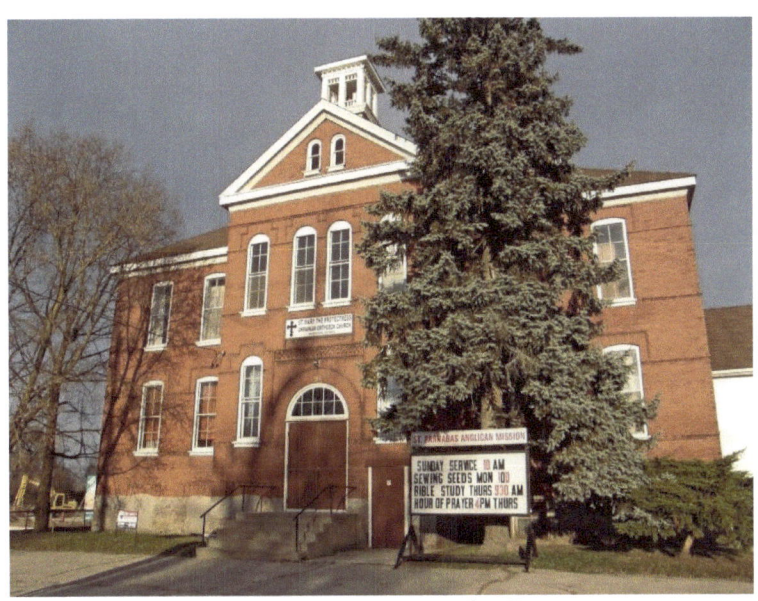

91 Bruce Street - St. Mary the Protectress
Ukrainian Orthodox Church

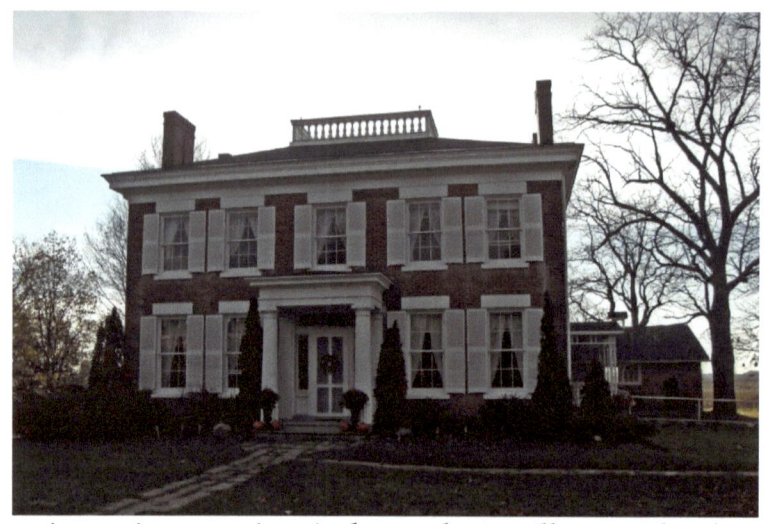

Georgian – six-over-six windows, doric pillars, widow's walk
on rooftop, sidelights and transom window around door

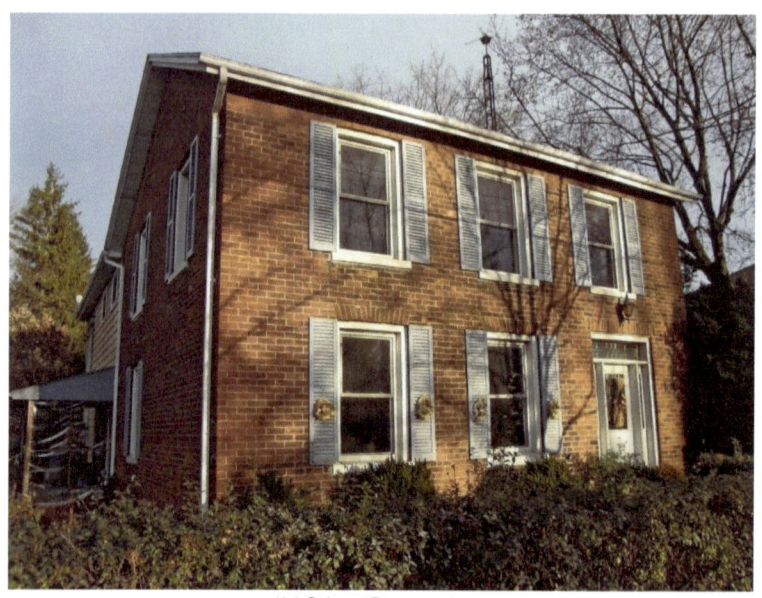

#101 - Georgian

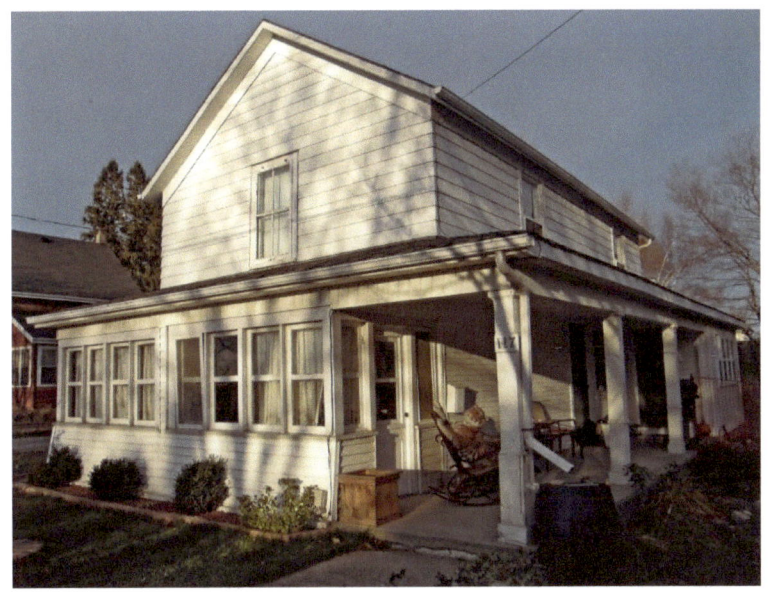

#117

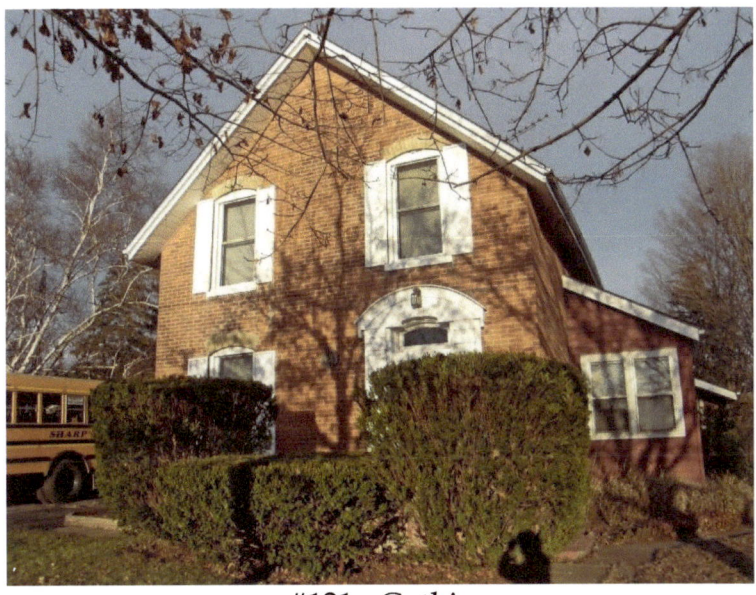

#121 - Gothic

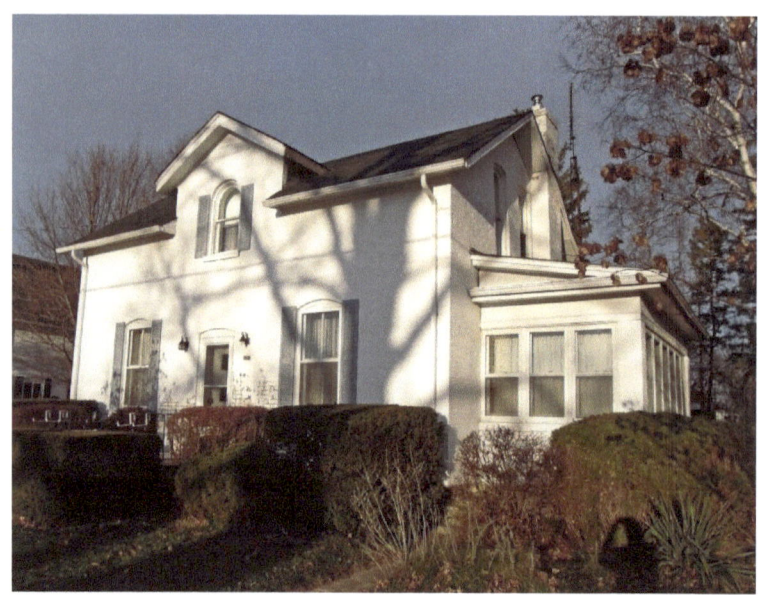

#127

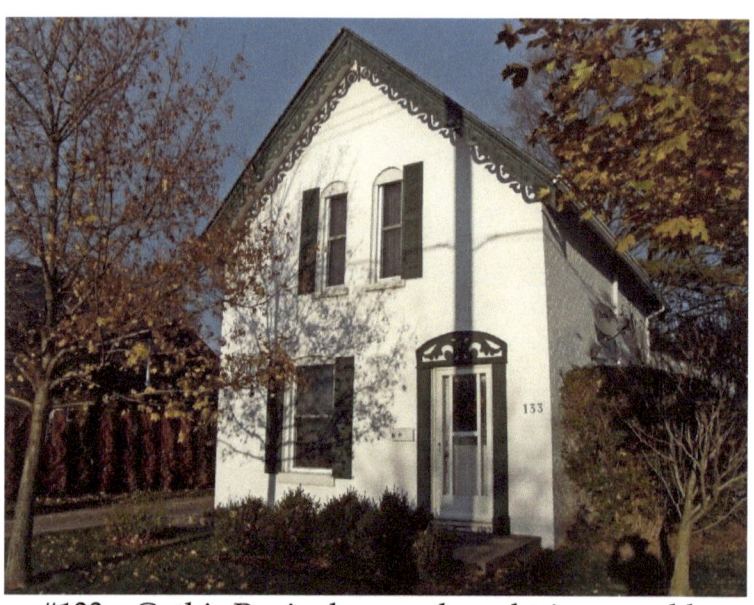

#133 – Gothic Revival, verge board trim on gable

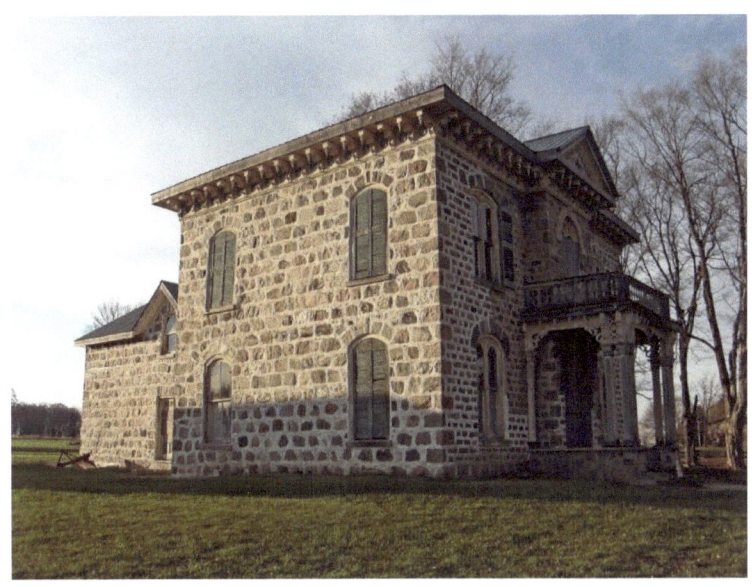

Stan Pajor, Dundurn, Ontario Farm

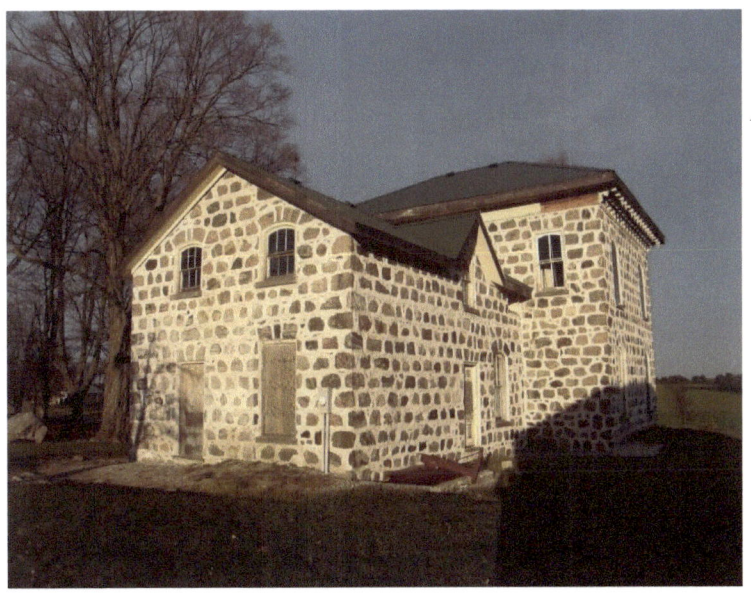

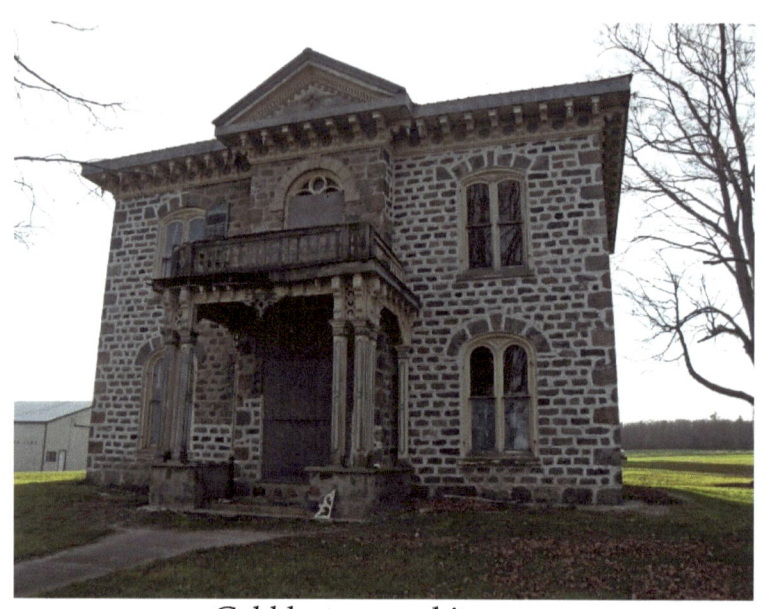

Cobblestone architecture

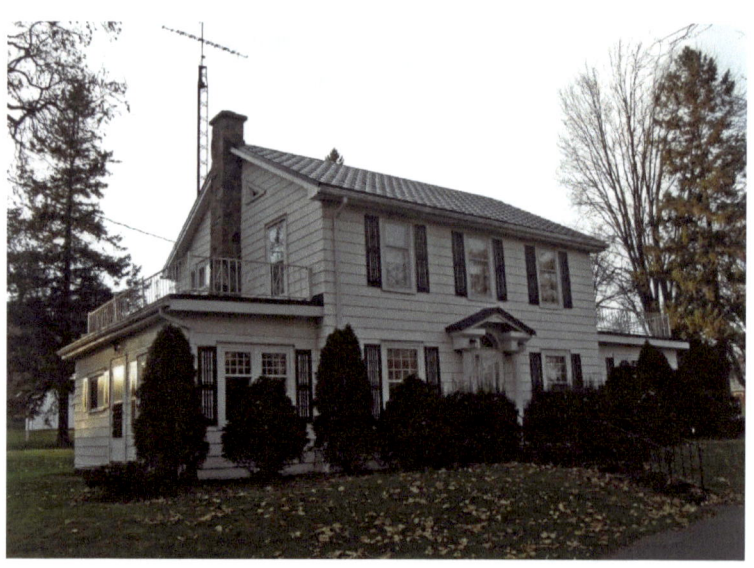

Ohsweken

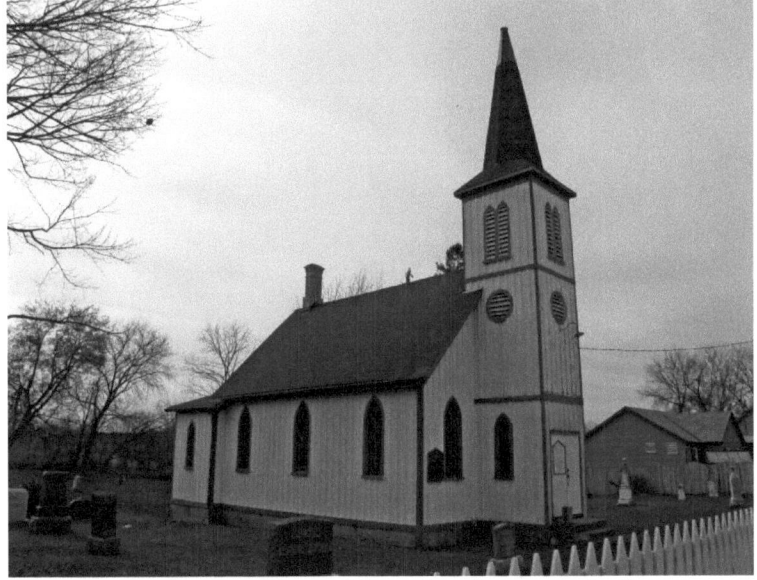

St. Paul's Anglican Church – lancet windows

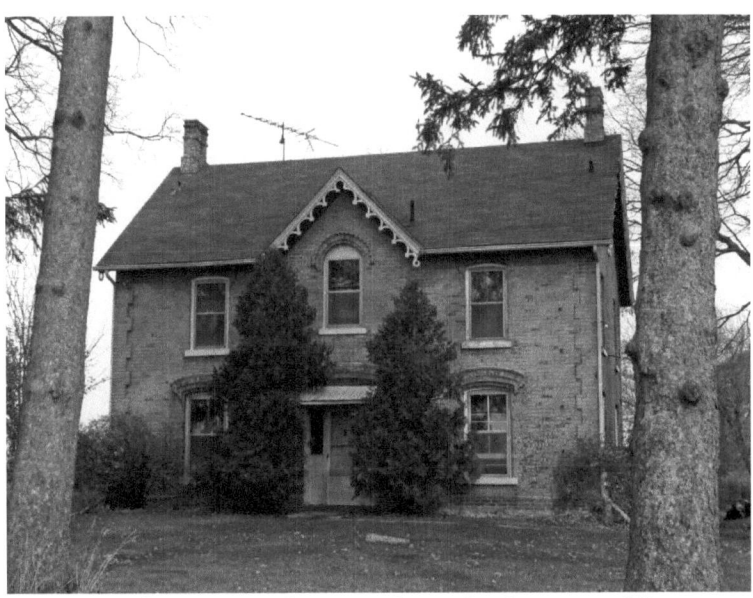

Gothic Revival, verge board trim on gable

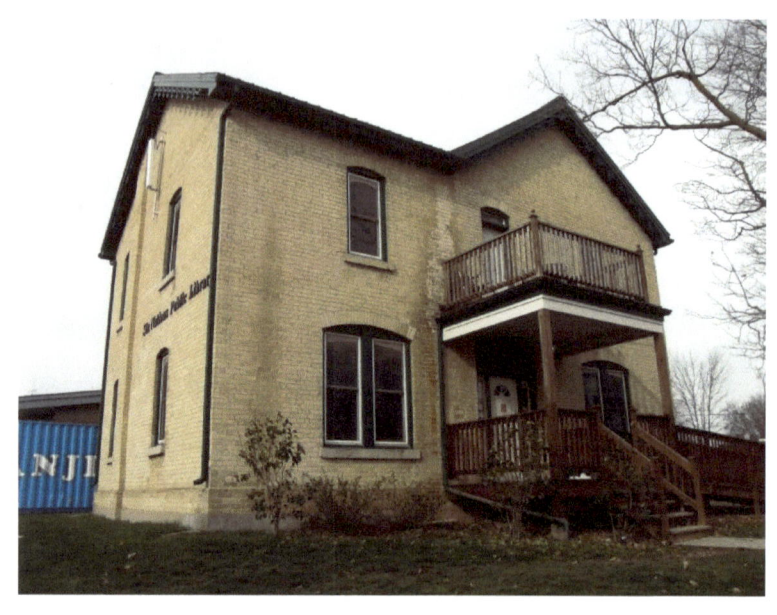

Six Nations Public Library

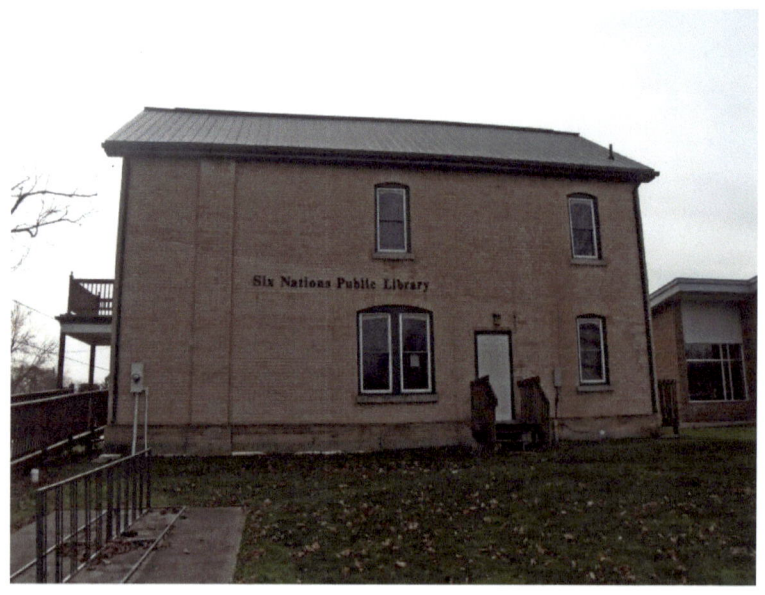

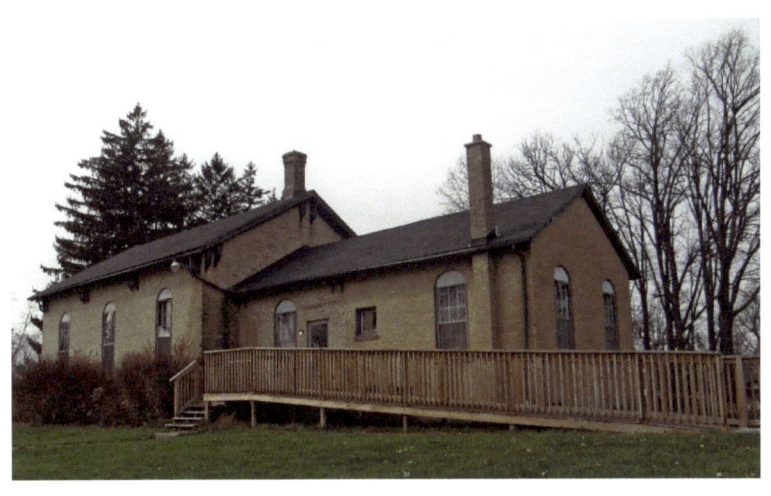

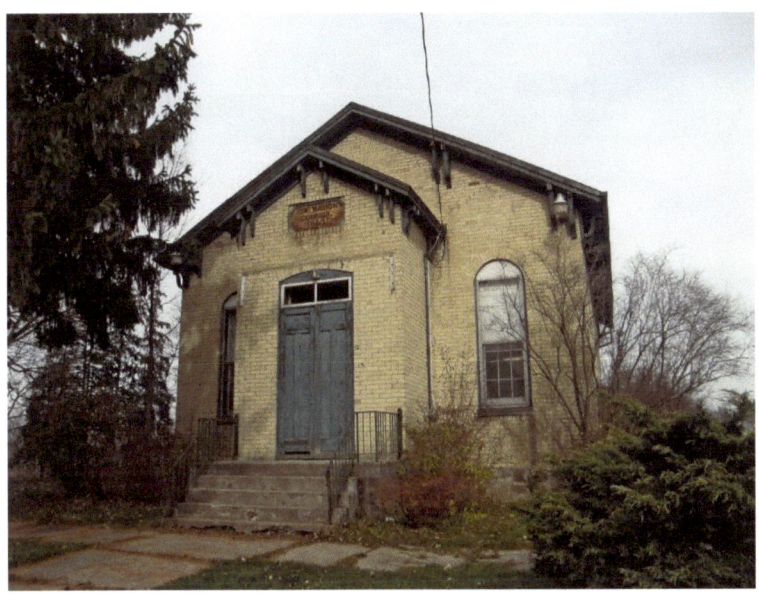

Six Nation Council 1863

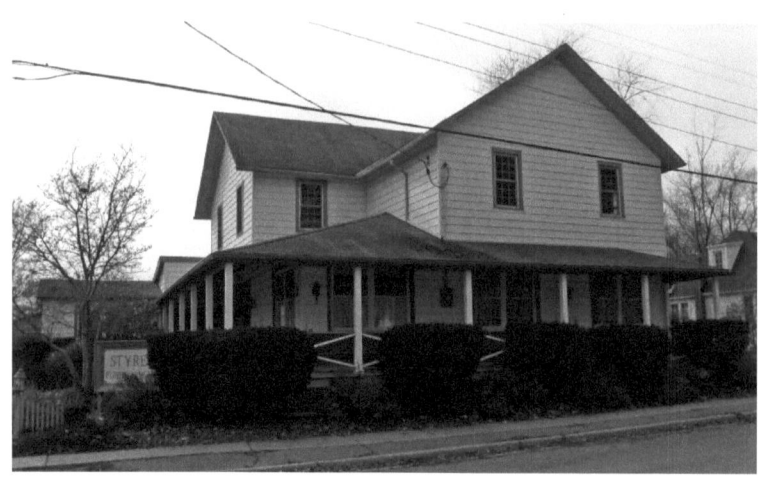

Styres Funeral Home

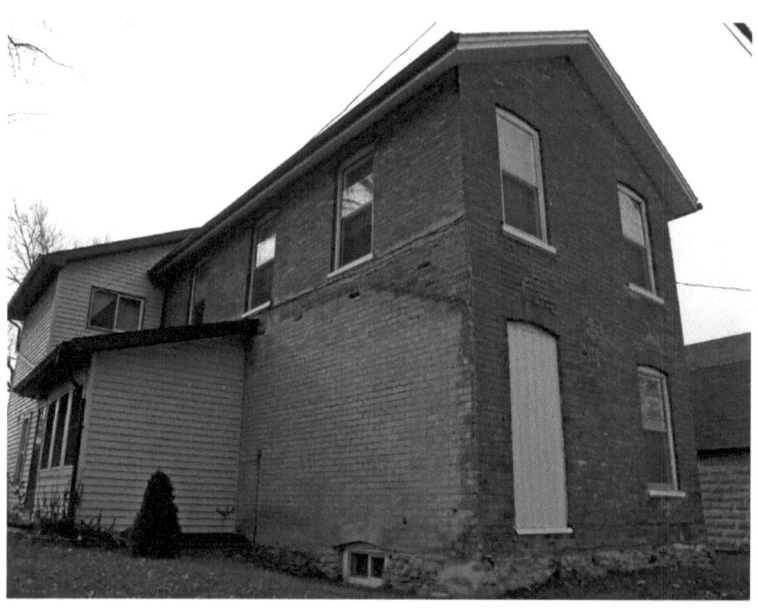

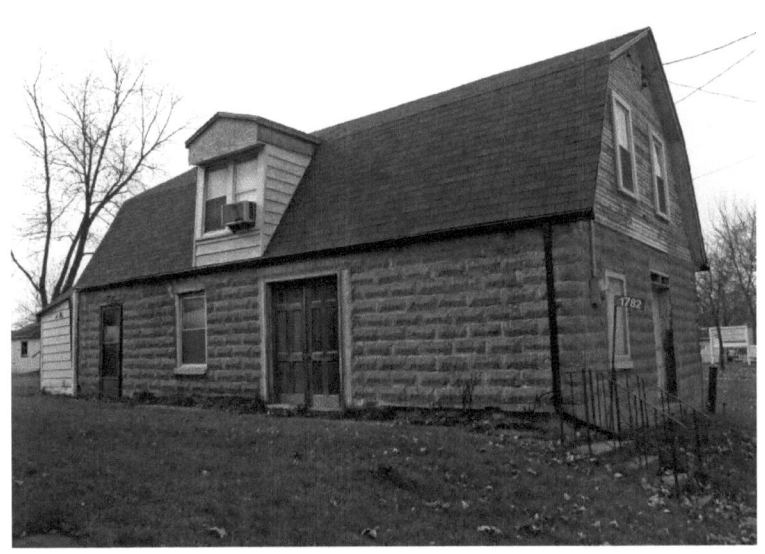

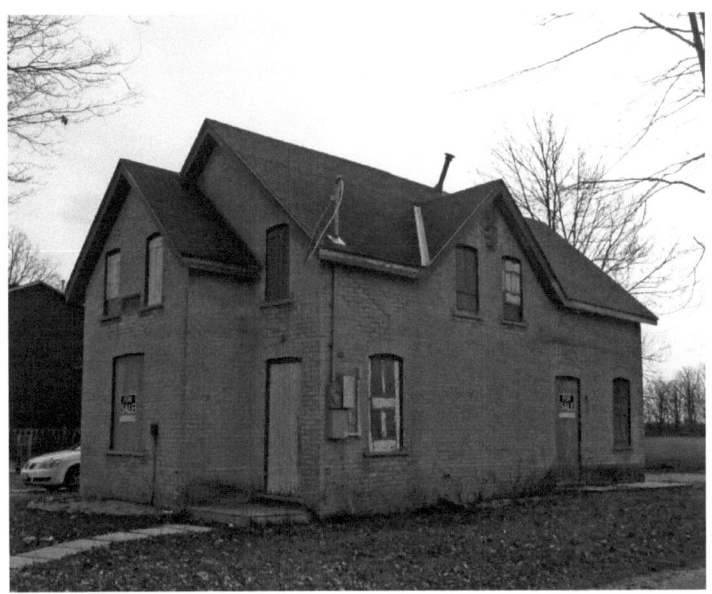

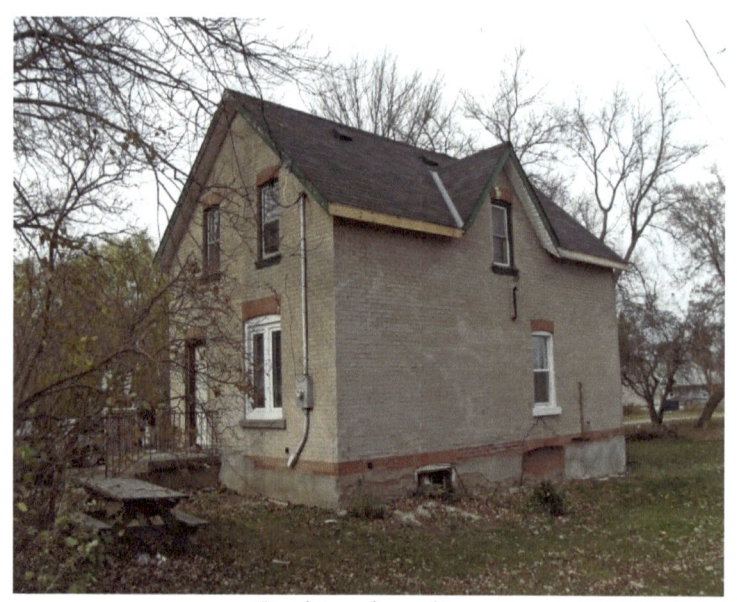

Gothic - banding

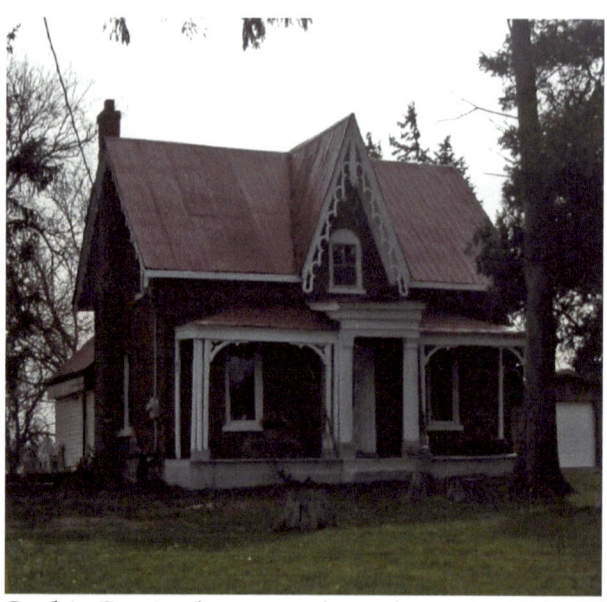

Gothic Revival – verge board trim and finial

Hartford

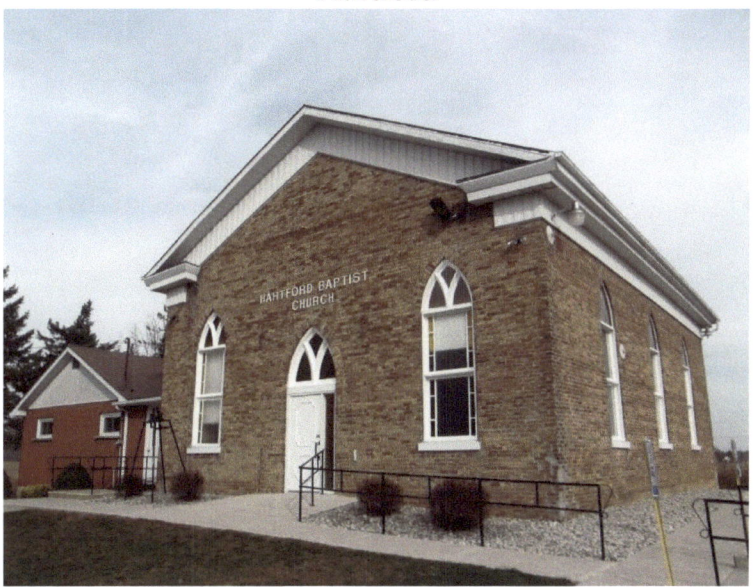

2700 County Line 74 -
Hartford Baptist Church – established 1834
Cornice return on gable

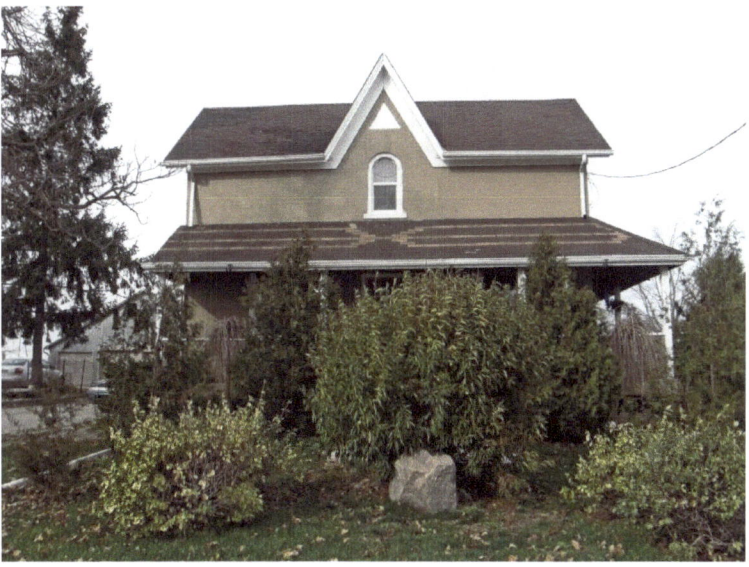

Gothic

Bealton

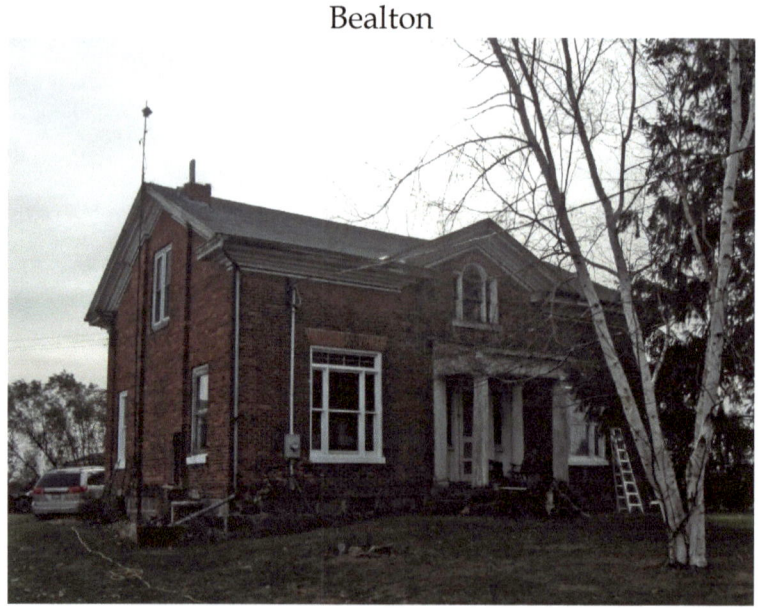

Gothic

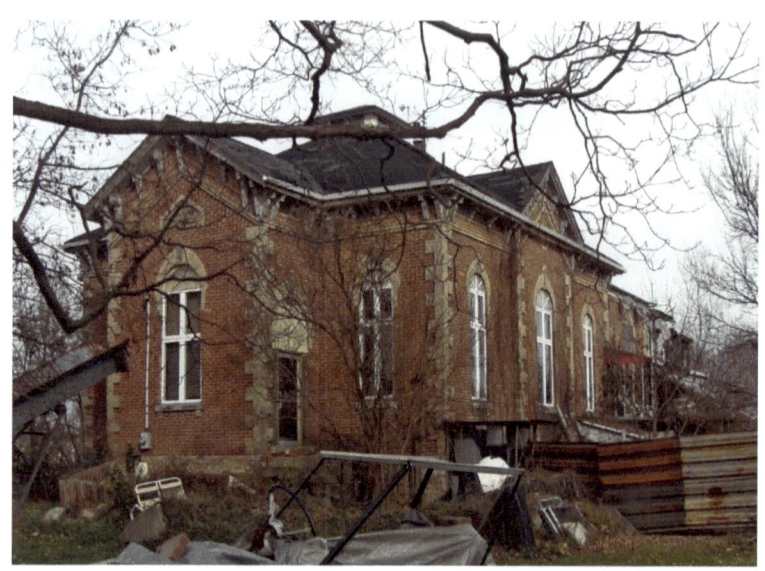

Corner quoins, cornice brackets

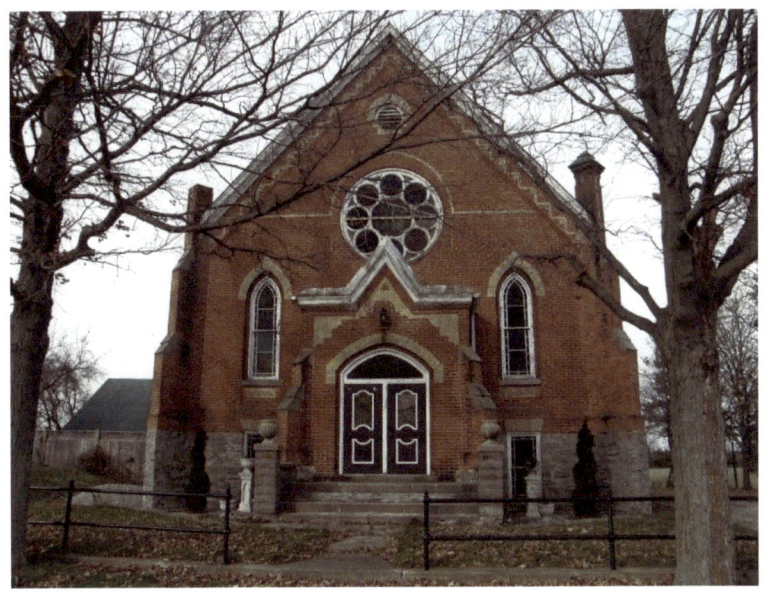

Methodist Church 1890 – rose window, dichromatic
brickwork, lancet windows

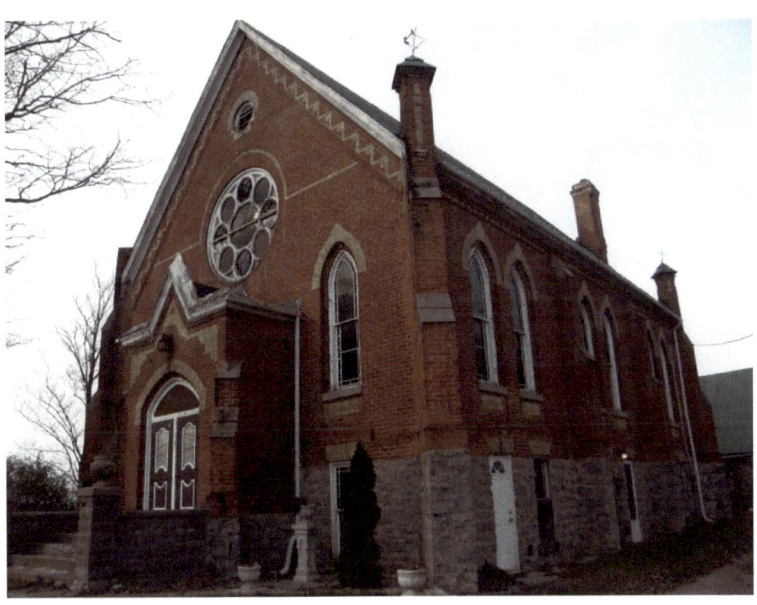

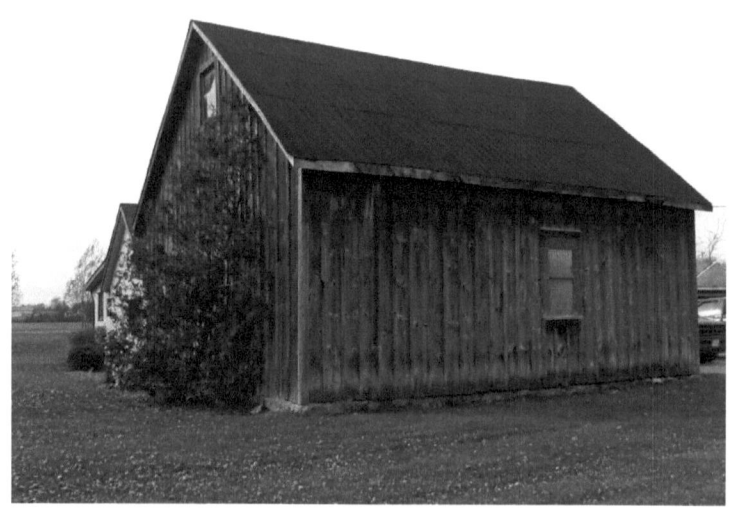

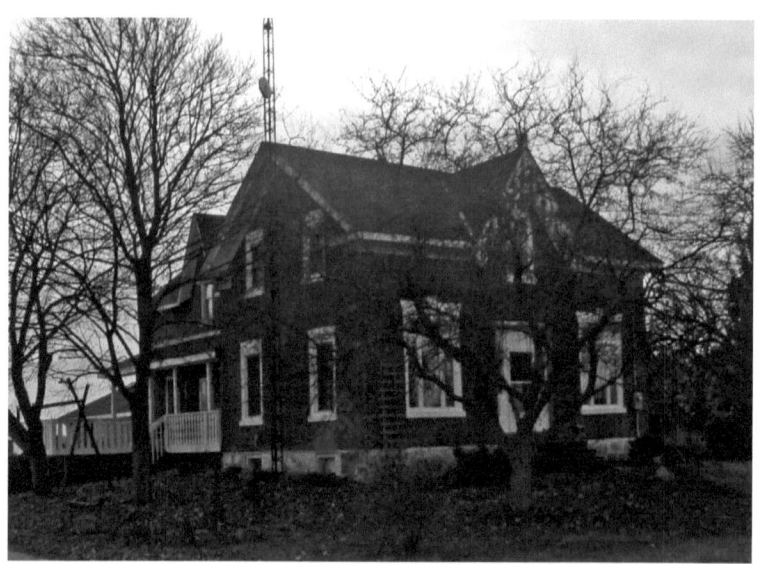

Gothic Revival

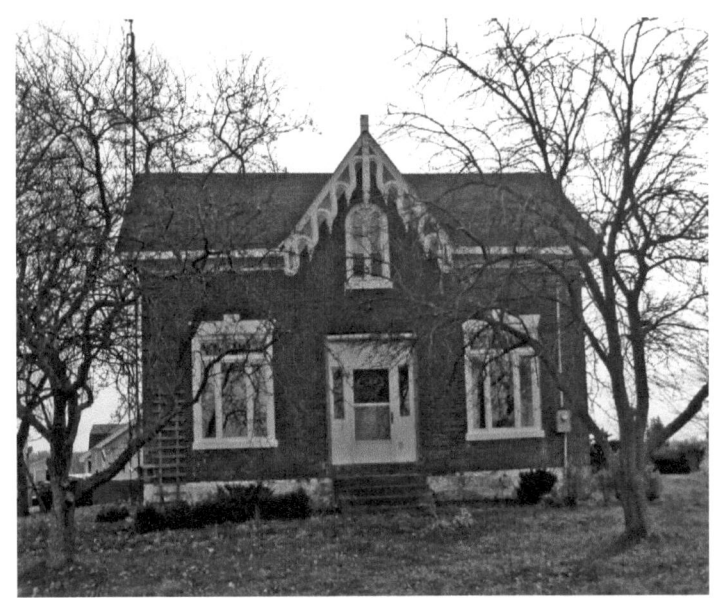

Gothic Revival – verge board trim and finial on gable

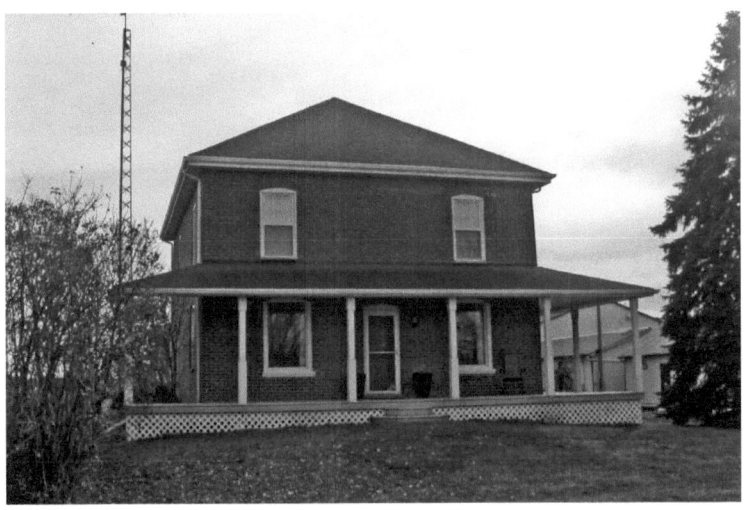

Hipped roof

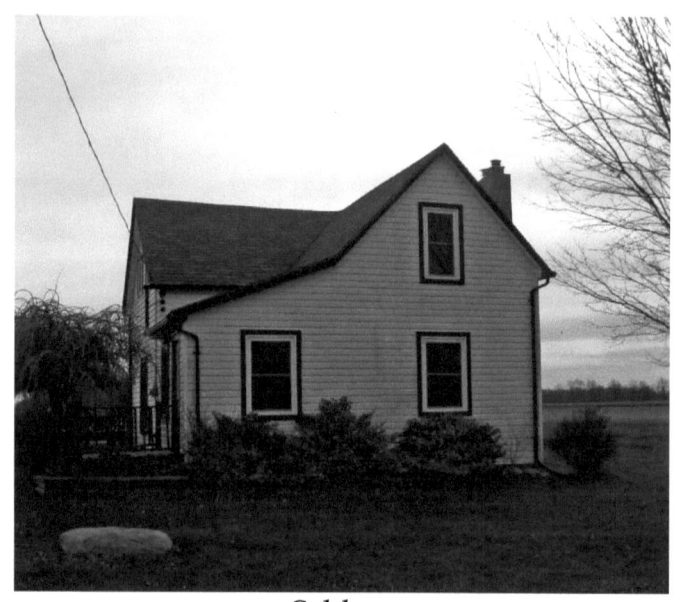

Saltbox

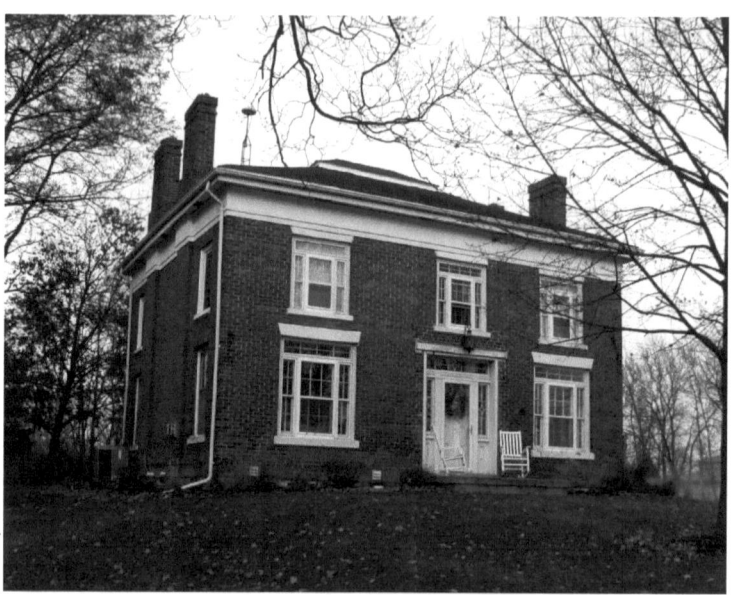

Italianate – hipped roof

Boston

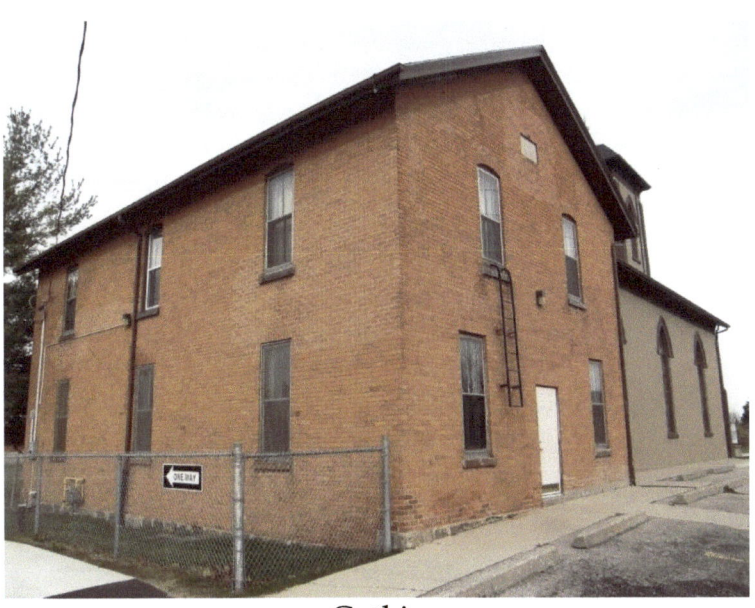

Baptist Chapel 1851

Gothic

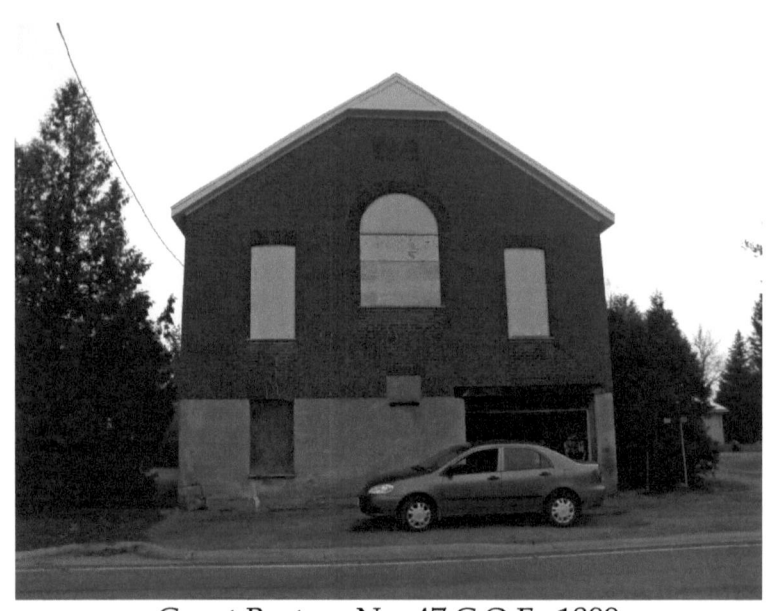

Court Boston, No. 47 C.O.F., 1899

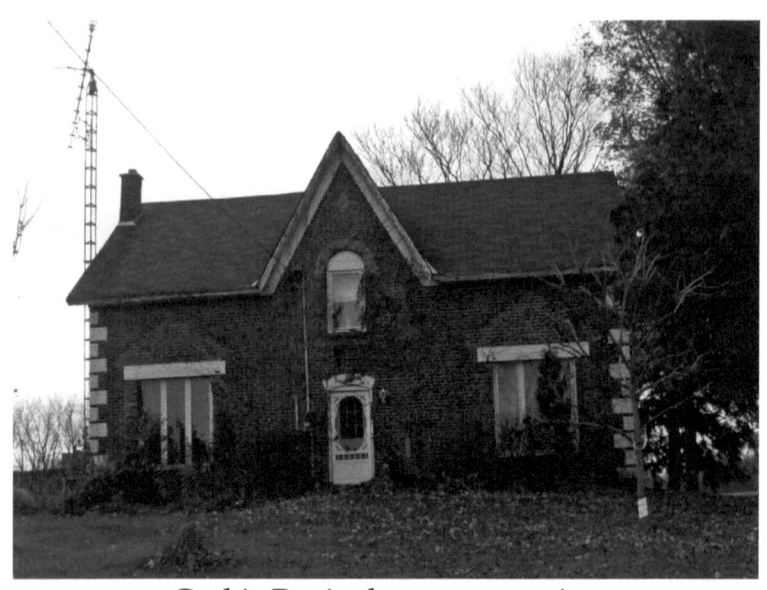

Gothic Revival – corner quoins

Oakland

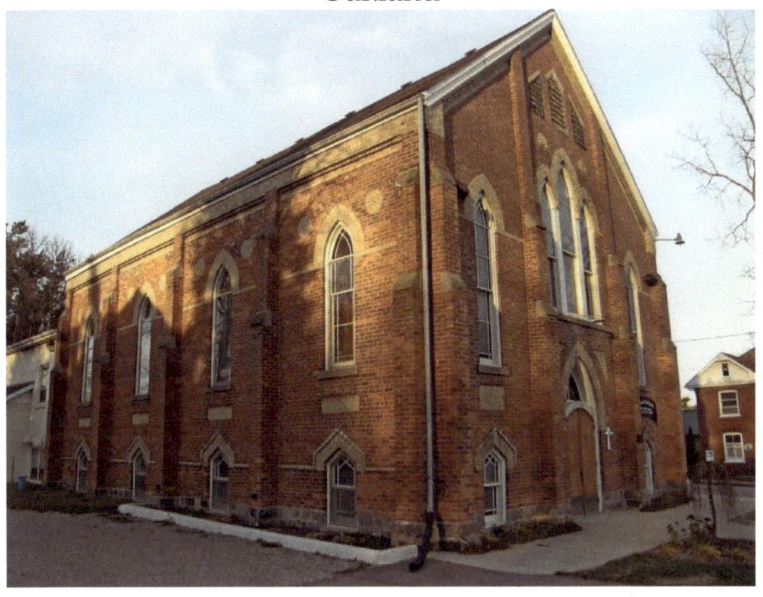

154 Oakland Street - Oakland United Church
(Former Methodist Church 1886)

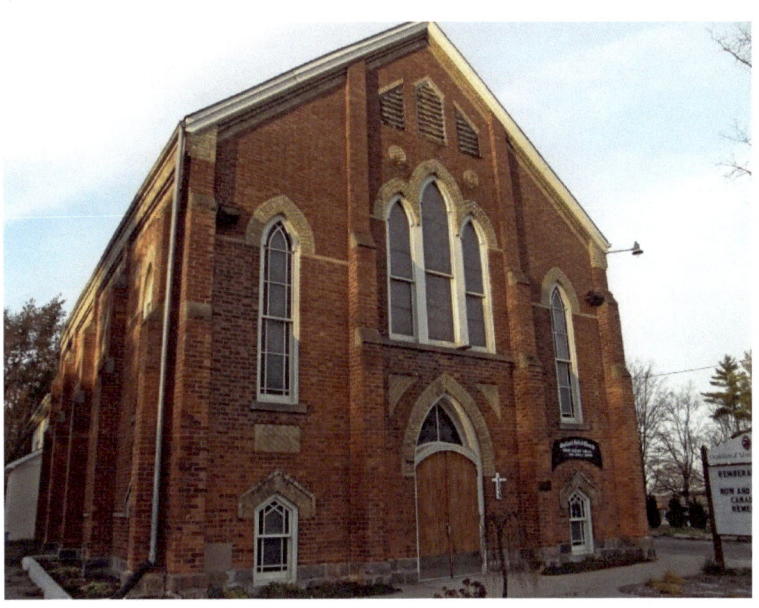

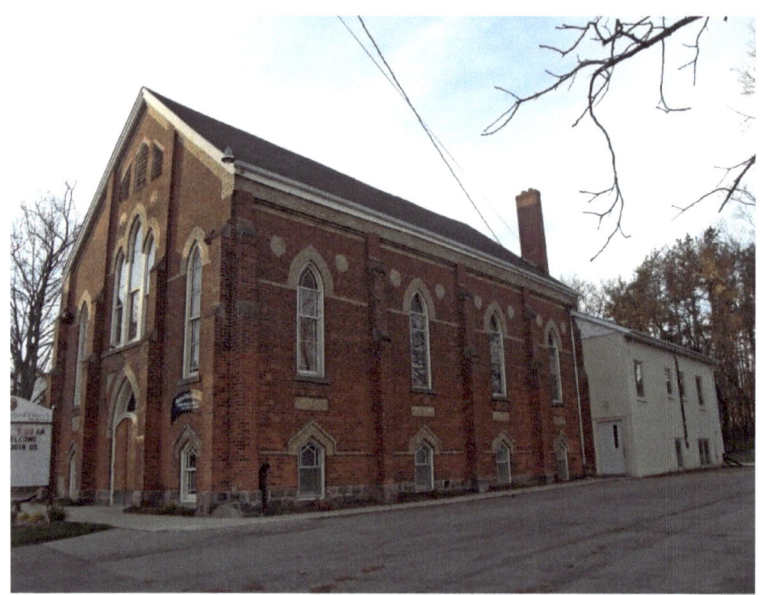

Gothic Revival, lancet windows, dichromatic brickwork

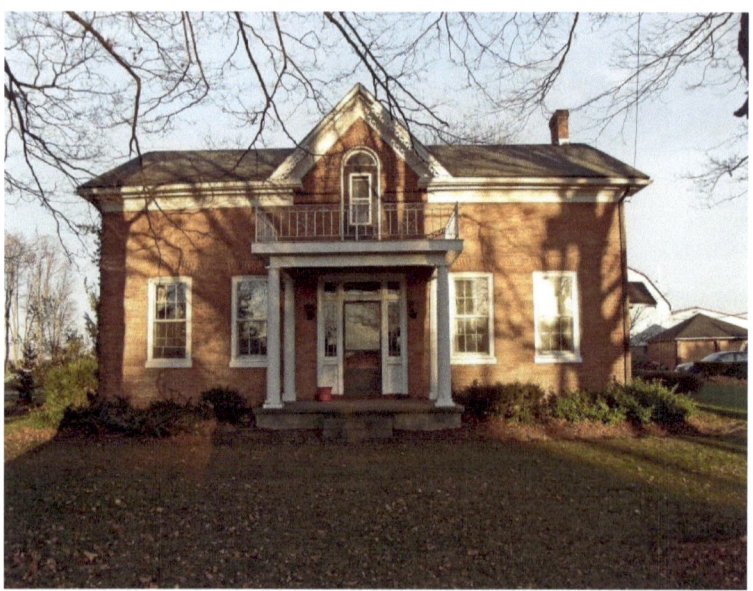

Gothic Revival

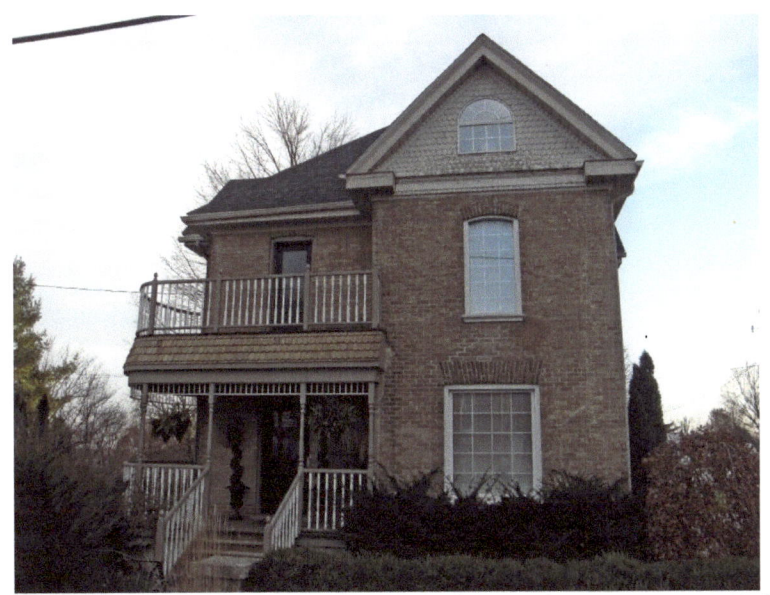

Edwardian – cornice return on gable, 2nd storey verandah

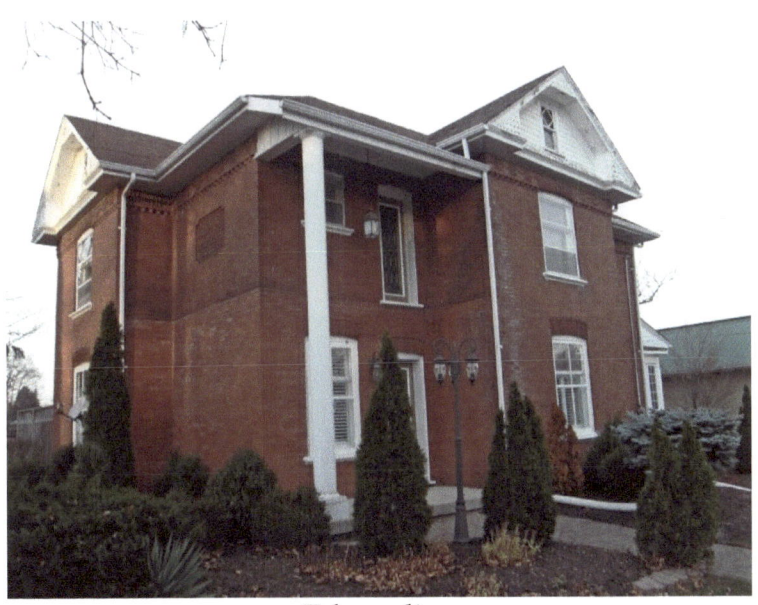

Edwardian

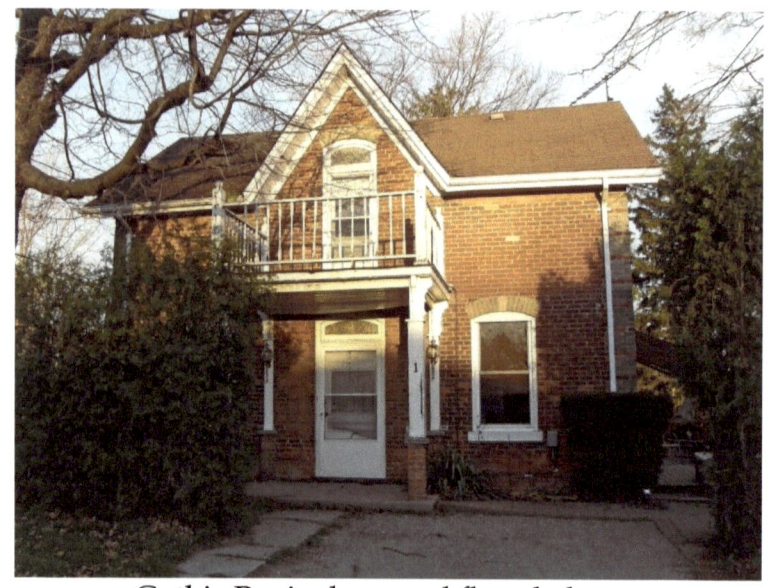

Gothic Revival, second floor balcony

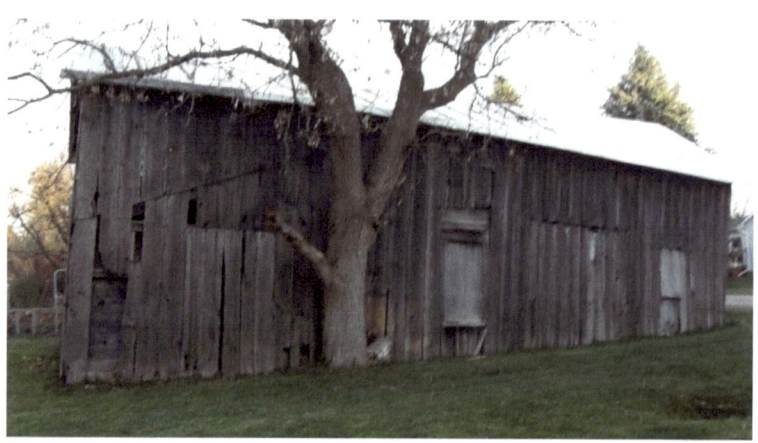

Old barn

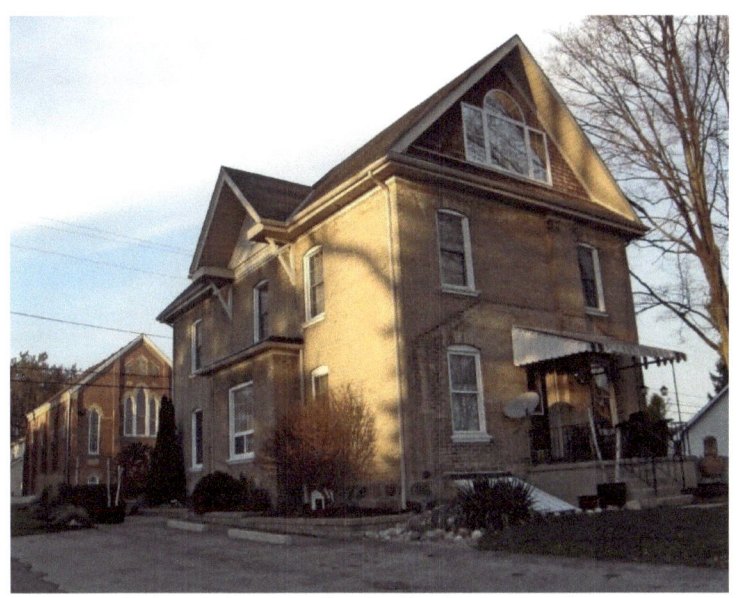

Edwardian style, Palladian window

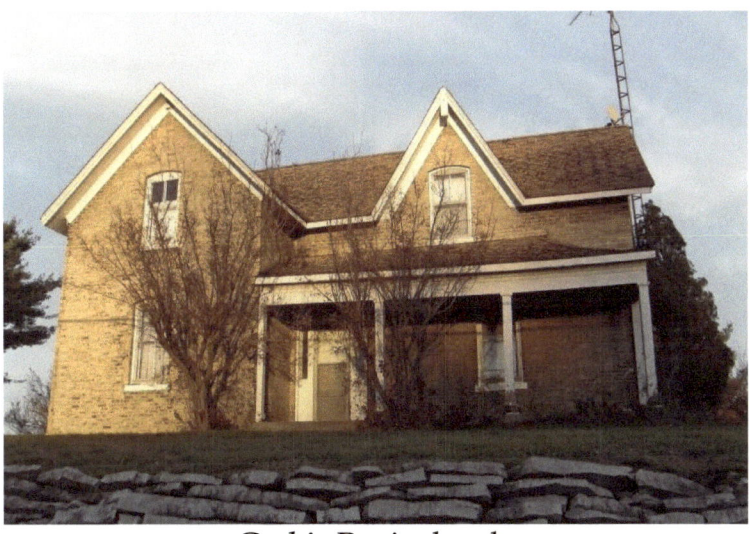

Gothic Revival style

Architectural Terms

Belvedere: (from the Italian "beautiful view") an architectural feature on a roof, in a garden or on a terrace that gives a beautiful view. Example: 92 Main Street, Waterford	
Brackets: a decorative or weight-bearing structural element which forms a right angle with one side against a wall and the other under a projecting surface such as an eave or roof. Example: Waterford, see Page 10	
Buttress: a masonry structure built against or projecting from a wall which serves to support or reinforce the wall. In Canadian architecture, they are sometimes used for decoration. Example: Waterford Baptist Church, Page 29	
Capital: The uppermost finish or decoration on a column. A Doric column is characterized by a plain column with no base, a shaft with twenty flutings, and a simple capital with a simple entablature. Example: Waterford, see Page 20	
Cobblestone architecture: Refers to the use of cobblestones embedded in mortar as a method for erecting walls on houses and commercial buildings. Example: see Page 39	

Cornice: originally the wooden overhang of the roof. With the use of stone, brick, iron and steel, the cornice is any projecting shelf at the top of a ceiling or roof. They can be very decorative. Example: Waterford, Page 32	
Cornice Return: decorative element on the end of a gable. Example: Waterford, Page 35	
Dentil Moulding: an even series of rectangles used as ornamental decoration in cornices. Example: Waterford Baptist Church, Page 29	
Dichromatic brickwork: the use of two colours of brick, tile or slate to decorate a façade. Example: Methodist Church, Bealton, Page	
Dormer: (French for "sleep") a gable end window that pierces through the plane of a sloping roof surface to create usable space in the top floor or attic of a building by adding headroom. Example: Waterford, see Page 7	
Gable: the triangular portion of a wall between the edges of a sloping roof. Example: Waterford, see Page 7	

Hipped Roof: a roof where all sides slope downwards to the walls with no gables. Example: Bealton, see Page 51	
Keystones and Voussoirs: a voussoir is a wedge-shaped element used in building an arch. A keystone is the central stone that locks all the stones into position, allowing the arch to bear weight. A keystone is often enlarged and embellished. Example: Waterford, see Page 21	
Lancet Window: a tall, narrow window with a pointed arch at its top. Example: St. Paul's Anglican Church, Ohsweken	
Mansard Roof: This style was popularized by Francois Mansart (1598-1666), an accomplished architect of the French Baroque period and especially fashionable during the Second French Empire (1852-1870). This roof is almost flat on the top section, with two slopes on each of its sides with the lower slope at a steeper angle than the upper and having dormer windows. Example: Waterford, see Page 21	
Palladian Window: a large window that is divided into three sections with the centre section larger than the two side sections and usually arched. Example: Oakland, see Page 59	

Pediment: a triangular section above the horizontal structure (entablature), typically supported by columns. The inside of the triangle is called the tympanum. Example: 163 Main Street, Waterford, Page 13	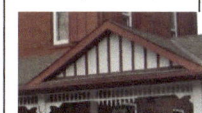
Quoin: masonry blocks at the corner of a wall, often a decorative feature, usually larger or of a different colour than the rest of the wall. Example: Bealton, see Page 48	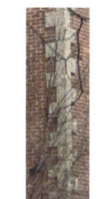
Rose Window: a circular window with ornamental tracery radiating from the centre. Example: Methodist Church, Bealton, Page 49	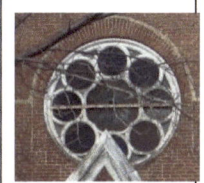
Sidelight: a window, usually with a vertical emphasis, that flanks a door, and is often used to emphasize the importance of a primary entrance. **Transom Window:** the light above the doorway, also called a fanlight. Example: Waterford, see Page 36	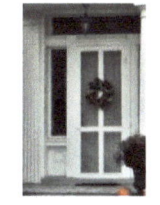
Turret: a small tower that projects from the wall of a building. Example: Waterford, see Page 13	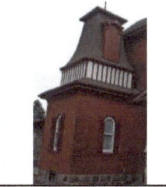
Verge board and Finial: also called bargeboards – hang from the projecting end of a roof and are often elaborately carved and ornamented. **Finial:** ornament added to the top of a gable, pinnacle, canopy or spire – a Gothic element. Example: 181 Main Street, Waterford	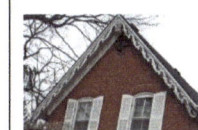

Cape Dutch architecture is a traditional Afrikaner architectural style found mostly in the Western Cape of South Africa. The initial settlers of the Cape were primarily Dutch. When the Dutch came to Ontario, they brought with them building concepts from their own native lands. Architecture from the 18th and early 19th centuries in Ontario includes a wide assortment of detailing and ornament all applied to a basic building design centred around the fireplace and the source of water. Example:	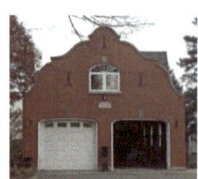
Georgian, before 1860 – This style began with the British King Georges in the 18th century. These buildings have balanced facades around a central door, medium-pitched gable roofs, and small paned windows. Example: Waterford, Page 36	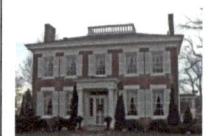
Gothic Revival, 1830-1890 – These decorative buildings have sharply-pitched gables with highly detailed verge boards, pointed-arch window openings, and dichromatic brickwork. It is a common style in Ontario. Example: Waterford, Page 38	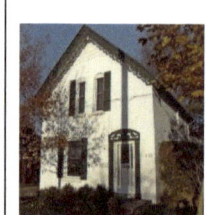
Italianate, 1850-1900 – It has wide-bracketed eaves, belvederes, wrap-around verandahs. Example: 138 Main Street	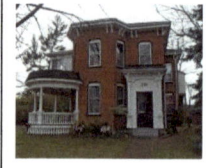

Queen Anne, 1885-1900 – This style is distinguished by an irregular outline featuring a combination of an offset tower, broad gables, projecting two-storey bays, verandahs, multi-sloped roofs, and tall, decorative chimneys. A mixture of brick and wood is common. Windows often have one large single-paned bottom sash and small panes in the upper sash. Example: Waterford, see Page 22	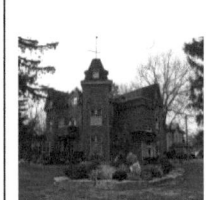
Saltbox: A saltbox is a building with a long, pitched roof that slopes down to the back, generally a wooden frame house. A saltbox has just one storey in the back and two stories in the front. The asymmetry of the unequal sides and the long, low rear roof line are the most distinctive features of a saltbox, which takes its name from its resemblance to a wooden lidded box in which salt was once kept. The earliest saltbox houses were created when a lean-to addition was added onto the rear of the original house extending the roof line sometimes to less than six feet from ground level. Example: Bealton, Page 52	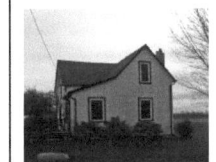
Second Empire, 1860-1880 – The mansard roof is the most noteworthy feature of this style and is evidence of the French origins. Projecting central towers and one or two-storey bays can also be present. Example: 160 Main Street, Waterford	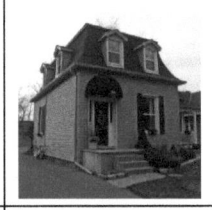
Tudor Revival – exposed timbers with stucco infill, multi-paned windows. Example: 156 Main Street, Waterford	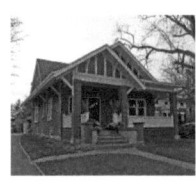